Praise for *Discover Your CEO Brand*

"Smart, practical, snappy, engaging, sophisticated, and wise. Bates has written a brilliant book . . . read . . . learn . . . enjoy . . .
— Ned Hallowell, author, *Shine, Driven, to Distraction,* and *Delivered from Distraction*

"Suzanne Bates book is fast paced, engaging, and chock full of valuable, practical lessons on how to build and manage your brand. It's a must read for all entrepreneurs."
— Aileen Gorman, Executive Director
The Commonwealth Institute

"Engaging and compelling reading for every executive who needs a formula to communicate who you are and what you are all about."
— Ellen Lord, General Manager
Textron Defense Systems

"Brand is a critical element of both personal as well as organizational success. In her amazing new book, Discover Your CEO Brand, *Suzanne Bates not only crystalizes why leaders must develop their personal brand, she also lays out a comprehensive approach as to how to accomplish this critical objective. This just may be Suzanne's finest work to date."*
— Larry Bonfante, CIO, United States Tennis Association, Founder CIO Bench Coach, LLC, and author of "Lessons in IT Transformation"

"As CEO, your brand speaks volumes to your employees and customers. Here's a jam-packed playbook for propelling your brand and paving the way for a reputation revolution among those following your lead!"
— Kirk Davis, President, GateHouse Media Inc

Bates inspires you to embark on the journey of defining and promoting your brand in Discover Your CEO Brand. *She makes this journey accessible, enjoyable, and a must for any successful leader."*
— Paula Johnson, Executive Director, Connors Center, Chief Division of Women's Health, Brigham and Women's Hospital

"When you look at the most successful companies in the world there is always a 'branded' CEO out front promoting and campaigning. In Suzanne's latest book she cites case studies, checklists, and countless stories on what you need to do to find, develop, and hone your own unique brand. It is a MUST READ for any current or aspiring CEO."

—Rob Nixon, global consultant to the accounting profession

In her newest book, Suzanne Bates quotes Amazon founder Jeff Bezos as saying "You earn a reputation by trying to do hard things well." That's exactly what Suzanne does in this wonderfully engaging, step-by-step practical guide to developing a personal leadership brand. She tackles the hard thing of teaching executives how to build their own brands—and she does it exceedingly well. An inspiring coach and storyteller, Suzanne walks her readers through every step of the brand-building process. She examines all the personal and professional elements that go into building influence and, along the way, shares plenty of actionable advice, useful checklists, and real-world examples from dozens of famous CEOs and celebrities.

—Mary Fran Johnson, Editor-in-Chief
CIO magazine and events

"Branding is essential to the success of every CEO as well as every organization. This book is rife with stories of well-known CEOs, fast-track tips, exercises, and more to guide you through building your brand and leveraging it to propel yourself and your company. It's a must-read."

—Sheryl Lindsell-Roberts, author of 24 books, including New Rules for Today's Office Strategies for Success in the Virtual World

DISCOVER YOUR CEO BRAND

SECRETS TO EMBRACING
AND MAXIMIZING YOUR
UNIQUE VALUE AS A LEADER

SUZANNE BATES

New York   Chicago   San Francisco   Lisbon   London
Madrid   Mexico City   Milan   New Delhi   San Juan   Seoul
Singapore   Sydney   Toronto

1 2 3 4 5 6 7 8 9 10 DOC/DOC 1 6 5 4 3 2 1

ISBN 978-0-07-176286-1
MHID   0-07-176286-8

e-ISBN 978-0-07-176290-8
e-MHID   0-07-176290-6

McGraw-Hill books are available at special quantity discounts to use as premiums and sales promotions, or for use in corporate training programs. To contact a representative, please e-mail us at bulksales@mcgraw-hill.com.

This book is printed on acid-free paper.

To Mom and Dad

Contents

Acknowledgments

MANY PEOPLE HAVE HELPED SHAPE my understanding of the importance of the leader's brand. Others have supported me while I've been building a business, writing a book, and living a life. I'm deeply grateful to my husband, Drew Yanno, and daughter, Meghan McGrath. I also owe a debt of gratitude to the president of our company, Dave Casullo, and Dave's family for the sacrifices they make every day. This gratitude extends to the rest of our team: Maura Waxwood, Hazel Watkinson, Jay Ryan, Craig Bentley, Sarah Woods, Margery Myers, Paula Lyons, Joe Panepinto, and Shellie Dunlap for making it happen every day.

Thanks to my editor, Donya Dickerson, who has been my guide through all three books at McGraw-Hill, as well as some dear friends who work with our firm every day to help us communicate who we are and build our brand. Those include Ken Lizotte, Kate Victory Hannisian, Tara Frier, and Margrette Mondillo. I'm also grateful to members of my Million Dollar Club, especially Alan Weiss, as well as Chad Barr, Rob Nixon, Guido Quelle, Alan Fortier, and Andrew Sobel, and others in the Hall of Fame, who urged me to "be bigger."

I am indebted to all the members of my chapter of the Women Presidents Organization for their support, as well as my colleagues in the National Speakers Association, New England chapter, and Dan Dunlap, for teaching me about business management.

Thanks to people who have taught me the art of storytelling, including Lou Heckler, Patricia Fripp, and Marcia Reynolds. I want to acknowledge the great work of Doug Stevenson, a master storyteller. And I want to express my appreciation to all who helped secure interviews, including Jon Symons, Michelle Press, and Dave DeFillipo.

Finally, thanks to the outstanding leaders who agreed to share their stories, insights, and wisdom. I believe every reader of this book will benefit in many ways because you have chosen to tell your story.

Introduction

Character is like a tree and reputation like a shadow. The shadow is what we think of it; the tree is the real thing.

—Abraham Lincoln

WHAT IS A CEO BRAND? AND why do you need one? If you are picking up this book, you are curious about discovering your own brand. Perhaps you're also just a little skeptical. After all, if you are a leader, you put your organization first. Your job is to lead. Having your own brand may seem, well, indulgent. You may not have placed personal brand building at the top of your list.

In truth, a powerful leader brand is essential to your success and your company's future. By the time you've read this introduction, I think you'll see why it's so important to have a great brand. When you finish this book, you will have discovered your brand, and I believe you'll be excited about leveraging it to benefit your organization.

Your brand is in essence your reputation. Reputation is the most important asset you have in business. Surely, that reputation is the *perception* about who you are as a leader and a person. Your reputation isn't *who* you are but rather what others *believe* about you.

Your character is the tree. That tree has been shaped, and continues to be shaped, by its environment. Character-building moments have defined you as a leader and have made you strong. These moments, told through stories, are the essence of your leader brand; they form your unique character and personality. In this book you're going to discover precisely how you came by that character—the values and beliefs that define you.

One hundred and fifty years ago, *branding* wasn't a word associated with leadership, but Abraham Lincoln's words form the fundamental principle of this book. As the tree grows, the shadow of your reputation grows. In this book you're going to learn how to grow your reputation so that it has a positive impact on your career, your company, and the world around you.

Your brand, or reputation, cannot be manufactured. A successful brand is built on what is real and authentic about you. Authenticity is critical. People know an authentic brand when they see one. It gives you enormous influence, and it also enhances your company's reputation.

The first step to discovering your brand is to embrace the idea that you have a brand, that it has power, and that you can harness it for the good of the enterprise. Let's start with some examples of how leaders have discovered and built their leader brands.

A BRAND LEGEND IN THE MAKING—ALAN MULALLY, FORD

When Alan Mulally took the helm at Ford Motor Company in 2006, he was not a likely choice. During a 37-year career at Boeing, he had been passed over twice for the CEO role. He had no experience in the automotive industry. Wall Street's reaction was tepid at best. William Ford, Jr., grandson of Henry Ford, was one of the few who believed Mulally was the right guy. Ford persuaded him to take over in the midst of major restructuring.

Inside Boeing, Mulally already had a brand, but it wasn't well known outside the industry. Still he had a brand—he was nothing if not intense, competitive, and committed to results. He oversaw the building of the Boeing 777. So, Ford Motor Company was about to find out about his commitment to a performance culture. Ford's chief financial officer, Lewis Booth, a 31-year Ford veteran, would soon tell reporters, "Alan's style is pretty relentless."

Mulally's character, the basis of his leadership brand, shaped the new culture of Ford. He became the driving force behind Ford's eventual, remarkable turnaround. His character was defined by both discipline and exuberance. He put in 12-hour workdays that started at 5:15 a.m. His energy and focus quickly became legendary and influenced the entire organization, reshaping the company culture. As his brand influenced the corporate dynamic, Ford came roaring back. It was the only car company to refuse federal bailout money, yet by 2010, it was turning a profit, increasing market share, and posting positive earnings.

Mulally reportedly once asked his mother, now 90, "Why am I this way?" She replied, "You've always been this way." Alex Taylor III, who writes for *Fortune* and covered Mulally for years at Boeing and then Ford Motor Company said, "He has given me his opinion on all the stories I've written about Ford since he took over and, for good measure, the stories I wrote about Boeing back when he worked there. The man . . . demands all my attention. He won't let up until he has turned all my 'nos' and 'maybes' into 'yeses.'"

How much was Mulally's powerful brand a factor in Ford's dramatic turnaround? Essential! It's undeniable. Many people didn't think there was a leader who could do it. In the hard-bitten automotive world, change has been hard. Long-tenured leaders and managers have been embroiled in turf battles. They have had tribe-like loyalties that have paralyzed business decisions. Could another leader have turned Ford around? Perhaps. But it is clear that Mulally's brand transformed the culture. He leveraged his style and reputation through a commitment to "communicate, communicate, communicate." That reinforced the right values and ignited the behaviors that quickly revived Ford and made it profitable once more.

WHAT IS THE VALUE OF A CEO BRAND? ASK STEVE JOBS

Mulally certainly isn't the first and only CEO whose brand has shaped and driven a company to unprecedented heights. Look at the value that Steve Jobs has created at Apple, the company he started in 1976. How do we know his brand has intrinsic value? Look at what happened in January 2011, when Jobs announced that he would be taking a third medical leave of absence. Although U.S. stock markets were closed when the announcement broke, in Frankfurt, Apple's shares immediately plunged by 6.4 percent. Think you can't measure the value of a leader's brand? It's as tangible as that.

We are not all Steve Jobs. We aren't all going to build iconic, multibillion-dollar enterprises. However, we can all take a page out of his book and others'. Each of us can have a commensurate impact on the value of our companies.

What has made Steve Jobs and Alan Mulally so formidable is the way they have leveraged the power of their brand values. There is more to their companies' successes than just good management and leadership practices. I am not suggesting these factors aren't critically important, but there is an additional, sometimes unrecognized, factor in a company's success—the leader's brand. A personal brand gives a leader "capital" he or she can expend to make things happen.

LEADER BRANDS ARE MADE, NOT BORN

Neither Mulally nor Jobs was born with a brand. Their brands developed as they became great leaders, and they grew stronger over time. Similarly, as you mature as a leader and discover what you stand for, you build a stronger, more durable, and valuable brand.

How does a leader's brand develop? Look at Jobs's story: When he was fired in 1985 from the company he founded, his brand actually took a major hit. When he returned in the late 1990s after a 12-year hiatus, he bought passion and commitment. He used newfound enthusiasm and love for innovation to rescue Apple from financial ruin and make it the iconic brand it is today.

HOW THIS BOOK WILL HELP YOU

How can you build a powerful leadership brand and leverage it for the benefit of your company?

That's what we're going to find out in this book. You will find powerful examples, and practical tools, that will help you to do these things:

- Discover your brand
- Understand how to use it

- Connect with key audiences
- Elevate your leader profile
- Use traditional/new media
- Attract and keep great talent
- Create business opportunity
- Shape a performance culture
- Drive value in your company

Jobs's brand was shaped by lessons hard won in his middle years when he was away from the company. He harnessed those lessons to drive incredible growth. Apple would soon go to market with some of the most innovative products of our time. The iPod, iPhone, and iPad have changed how we communicate and have altered the way we interact with technology.

How do you define the Steve Jobs's brand? It is elegant, useful, intuitive, technological innovation. He symbolizes the aesthetic sense that became Apple's DNA. His values shaped Apple in many ways. It attracted the right people who built the company into a powerhouse. They made Apple into a category of one in the industry. Anyone who has ever seen Steve Jobs on stage recognizes his remarkable platform skills. He engages his audience, commanding the room with passion and generating excitement about Apple's new products. Jobs embodies the Apple brand. He is the creator and the keeper of the brand. He is not just any chief executive. He is a brand—driving a brand.

HOW TO BECOME A BRAND—DRIVING A BRAND

You don't have to be Steve Jobs to bring tremendous value, to be a brand—driving a brand. The first step is to embrace the idea of building your own brand. In this book you'll find out how to do that. You'll also learn strategies for leveraging it for the benefit of your organization. You will discover your brand, understand how to use it, and communicate it to the world.

By investing time in reading this book, you'll have the tools to truly leverage your reputation for the good of your company, and you will feel more passionate than ever about doing so. Your brand, built on the values and principles that define you, will become an asset—like gold. And you'll feel even more confident about communicating your unique, valuable brand to influence, inspire, motivate, and persuade others to act.

Why is that important to your company? A great company brand deserves a great CEO brand! Whether you are the CEO, leader of a team, or hope to be someday, your brand is part of the company's brand package. A leader's reputation is an essential component of the corporate brand equation.

Some CEO brands add more value than others. As we'll see in Chapter 9, some CEOs actually detract from their company brands. But there's no question that, like it or not, every CEO has an impact on his or her company's brand, whether you're a company of one or one hundred thousand.

This book will help you get clear about who you are as a leader, what you believe, and how that defines your brand. Even if you already know a lot about your values, we're going to go deeper, to find the authentic, unique, and powerful leader brand inside you. This process is the foundation of the work we've done with leaders. I have seen how this exciting process can transform people into passionate leaders who love their work and love their lives.

Once you know your brand, you can use it, and amplify it, to achieve your goals. The simple steps in this book will help you to create a plan to communicate your brand. I'll also talk about how to build a team of people who will make you successful. The outcome will be no less than discovering what your leadership is all about, and how you can be most influential.

IS A BRAND ABOUT CELEBRITY?

In writing this book, I don't mean to imply that you should build a brand to become a global celebrity. Your goals are your goals; your dreams are your dreams. You will build a brand and bring value to your company in your own way. The tools in this book will help you do that.

The stronger your brand is with the audiences that matter, the easier it is to accomplish great things. It's easier to drive your vision forward, attract attention, influence people, hire great talent, align people around your plan, win trust, and deliver results. A bigger brand makes you more influential. You have to define what *big* means to you.

BRAND AND INFLUENCE

Many of our corporate clients ask, "How can we make our leaders more influential? How can we teach them the skill of influence?" Influence is not really a skill, although it requires skill. Influence is who you are and how you are perceived by others. It is vital to be skilled at communicating in an influential way, to understand how others think, how to connect with them, and how to persuade them.

These interpersonal skills alone do not make you an influential leader. You probably know people who have persuasive skills; these skills alone don't make them *leaders*. Leaders have a brand based on authentic values they use to influence others. Brand is the core of who you are as a leader and how you are perceived. When this core is strong and you know how to wield your reputation, you are an influential leader.

BRAND IS FOR EVERY LEADER

Building a brand is for any leader who wants to be successful. Even if you never want to become the CEO, if you are a leader, you need a brand. Your brand will help you attract the right people to your team; align them around a common purpose; mediate issues; get things done across the matrix of the organization; influence your CEO, board, and executive committee; and also help you create a more dynamic, high-functioning organization. Your brand will help you to win trust, create legions of fans, attract new opportunities, and advance in your career.

In this book you'll find examples of well-known leaders, as well as other leaders you don't yet know who have built powerful brands in their fields or industries. Some of the examples are household names; some of them aren't. All have great brand stories to share. We won't all be Warren Buffett or Richard Branson or Oprah Winfrey someday, but we can learn their secrets and the secrets of others who value and leverage their own leadership brands.

My goal is to share the underlying principles at work and help you as you build a brand that is respected and admired. You'll learn how to make the most of your brand and even measure the results of the impact your brand has.

One common characteristic of the hundreds of outstanding leaders I have coached, interviewed, and researched is that they have thought about their brands (even if they didn't call themselves a "brand") and they have figured out how to use that brand as a valuable asset in their careers. They understand, consciously or unconsciously, the value that their personal brand brings to their companies.

Through their stories you'll probably see yourself. Just like you, these leaders have been on a journey. They have lived a life. They have learned lessons. They have become interesting leaders with a unique perspective and certain skills and abilities that make them shine. Their lessons have shaped who they have become. Just like you, they've had life experiences that have given them a viewpoint and a set of values that make them the leaders they are today.

In essence, we're going to look at the story of you and the lessons from those stories that have made you who you are. I hope you'll be inspired to think about your own life and career in a new, exhilarating way. I hope this book will reenergize you and reignite your passion for leadership. And, I hope you'll use what you learn to build value into your company through your powerful brand.

HOW CAN YOU CLEARLY DEFINE YOUR BRAND TO OTHERS?

As the CEO, you embody the company brand. You are the face and voice of the organization. To clearly define your brand, you need to understand it. You can only define it for others if you're clear about it yourself. This means looking at your own life and experiences to discover the lessons and values that have shaped you and made you who you are.

In the chapters ahead we'll look at how other leaders, just like you, have looked at their own lives and careers for the clues that define their brands. We'll also explore how to examine your own stories and understand precisely what they are teaching you about yourself.

Our clients find that this process is exciting and rewarding. While some have spent more time than others analyzing the events that have shaped them, it is easier than you imagine to look at their life story and see what it is telling them.

As you begin this process, I recommend that you enlist help from an executive coach, mentor, or trusted advisor. If you want to get there quickly, it is easier and more productive to explore your brand with a partner who has your best interest at heart. In case you haven't identified that person, the exercises are designed so you can do them on your own. I strongly encourage you as you read the book to do the exercises. It's really the best way to truly gain insights that will allow you to define your brand.

HOW TO USE THIS BOOK

- The best way to use this book is as a guide, inspiration, and a practical tool. As you read the stories of leaders who have built great brands, think of your own story and of how those people's journeys can guide you. Be inspired by how they have discovered the values and principles that define them as leaders. Then, use the practical tools and exercises to explore your story, discover your brand, communicate it in a powerful way, and leverage it for great results.

- If you use the book this way, you will discover that platinum leadership brand inside you, and you'll be able to use it to your advantage to see greater success in your career and better results for the company. Whether you're a CEO or you want to be a leader someday, no matter how large or small your company, these exercises are powerful. They will help you shape the story of your leadership and ultimately start thinking about your legacy.

- I recommend that you read this book from beginning to end, whether all at once or a little at a time. If you're the kind of person who likes to skip around, by all means, start with a chapter that interests you, and then come back to the beginning to uncover the story of you and allow your brand identity to unfold. There will be chapters you'll want to revisit as you put together your brand plan.

- The chapters are organized as a step-by-step guide; one does provide context for the next. They also stand alone. I really encourage you to do the exercises. Invest in the self-discovery. Make it real for you. It is often tempting to keep reading, but if you skip the self-discovery, you will not receive as much value. I also encourage you not to make assumptions about your brand. Look at your stories to find a deeper richness. You may clarify things you never really knew about yourself, which is very exciting.
- Some leaders are best known for destroying their brands. In Chapter 9, we'll look closely at some famous brand disasters, and I encourage you to share this material with those on the brand team who support both the company and leader brand. Public relations, marketing, investor relations, speechwriters, and everyone involved in communicating the brand should pay particular attention to these lessons.
- Since none of us can do this alone, when you are ready to put your plan into action, you'll want to explore Chapter 10. That chapter offers advice and suggestions as to how to surround yourself with the people who support your brand. You'll need these people to make you look good. You'll also find some very practical exercises on communicating your brand through traditional media and social media in Chapters 7 and 8.

I hope you're excited about starting on this journey. Soon, you will be unlocking the brand inside you. When you close the book, I hope it is the start of a new chapter in your leadership life. My goal is for you to look back on the time you spent reading this book and doing the exercises as one of the best investments you've made in your career.

As an executive coach, a CEO, and an author who has researched and studied leaders, I'm excited to share this concept with you. My passion is helping executives become superb leaders. Your brand is a big part of that equation. This is a journey of self-discovery. It is also a practical business skill. What's exciting is to combine discovering who you are with driving value into your business.

So let's get started in Chapter 1 with how great leaders build brands that have value.

DISCOVER
YOUR CEO
BRAND

1

Why You Need a Brand—and Why Your Brand Matters

Who you are, what your values are, what you stand for. . . .
They are your anchor, your north star. You won't find them
in a book. You'll find them in your soul.

—ANNE MULCAHY, FORMER CHAIRMAN AND CEO, XEROX

THE CORE OF YOUR LEADERSHIP BRAND is who you are and what you stand for. You find it in your heart and your soul. The brand begins with the story of you—the experiences that defined you, the lessons you learned, and the ways those lessons shaped your values and beliefs. Once you understand the essence of your brand, you will be able to communicate it to the world. It will become a powerful force, creating positive results. You will be able to leverage that brand of yours to drive tremendous value into your company.

A brand is an intangible asset; however, the impact is very real. Smart, successful leaders put their brands to work and infuse the values represented by their brand into the fabric of their organizations. Your brand is a valuable asset you can leverage to create real results.

The essence of your brand—your character—is already well formed. The questions are, how well do you understand it, and how well is it communicated? What kind of impact could you have on your company and industry if you truly harnessed the power of your brand? In this chapter we'll look at why your brand is important. You will see how other leaders have employed the power of their brands to create value, and how you can do that, too.

The interesting feature of a leader's brand is that while it stands alone, it is also part of something larger. As the CEO or leader, you have your own *separate* brand, which also is commingled with the *organization's* reputation. So it stands to reason that you need to fully understand your own brand and also appreciate the interplay between your brand and your company's brand, so you can harness the two to work in concert. As you'll see in numerous examples in this chapter, a clearly defined leader brand can be a driving factor in a company's success.

You are an essential part of the overall corporate brand equation, helping shape the DNA of the company and ultimately driving performance. The first step to discovering your brand is to embrace the idea that you have a brand, that it has power, and that you can harness it to do great things. As you read the examples in this chapter, you'll see how other leaders have done that.

Throughout history there are many examples of CEOs who have built powerful brands that have added real, tangible value to their companies. In the sidebar, you'll see short examples of well-known leaders whose individual brands have defined corporate brands. Their beliefs and values have shaped the vision, future, and legacy of the enterprises.

Here are a *few* examples of famous brand-name leaders whose reputations and brand principles have driven value into their companies.

- **Walt Disney** had optimism and creativity, which were the driving forces behind his Hollywood success in animated feature films. His love of nature, family, and community inspired the Disney World and Disneyland amusement parks that became the cornerstone and symbol of the company's success.
- **Charles Merrill,** from humble beginnings, cofounded Merrill Lynch with a goal of helping the average investor navigate the markets. His belief in creating value for investors, and in the idea that everyone should know how to invest, made Merrill Lynch the largest brokerage in America.

- **Mary Kay Ash** launched her own cosmetic company after she was passed over for promotion in the company for which she worked, even though she was the highest seller there. Her success came from giving great sales incentives to consultants who earned them by being top sellers. She lived by the Golden Rule: treat others as you would want to be treated.
- **Lou Gerstner** masterminded one of the great turnarounds in corporate history in his nine years at IBM. When IBM was about to break up, his tough, direct, decisive style kept the company together.
- **Katharine Graham,** of the *Washington Post* fostered a culture of courage and perseverance, giving editors the autonomy that enabled the Watergate story to be told, forcing President Richard Nixon to resign.
- **Michael Dell** is an out-of-the-box thinker who hasn't been afraid to go his own way. His brainstorm to cut out the middle man in selling computers created a completely new business model, allowing Dell computers to become a wildly popular choice.
- **Oprah Winfrey** survived an abusive childhood and built a media empire on the philosophy of inspiring women to live their best lives. She rejected the typical tabloid-style entertainment in favor of promoting self-esteem and self-development.

Let's examine two other examples, Jack Welch, who led General Electric to become one of the largest most influential companies at the end of the last century, and Mark Zuckerberg, the founder of Facebook, a company that is altering the way we communicate in the new millennium. Think of them as being like Classic Coke and Vanilla Coke: two leader brands that have defined the very DNA of their organizations.

JACK WELCH, GENERAL ELECTRIC

The storied career of the man who would become the best-known CEO in America, *Fortune's* "Manager of the Century," is well documented. The son of a railroad engineer, Jack Welch was born and raised in Salem, Massachusetts, went to the University of Massachusetts, Amherst, and became a chemical engineer. He joined General Electric (GE) in 1960 at a salary of $10,500 a year. Relatively early in his career, he contemplated leaving GE, but a manager persuaded him to stay. Welch had definite ideas about the kind of company he wanted to be part of. In vintage style, he told his then-boss, "Well you are on trial."

Welch became GE's youngest CEO and chairman in 1981, and by then his well-formed personality became a force of nature. He streamlined the company and demanded efficiency, productivity, and quality control through Six Sigma. He insisted that GE should be number one or number two in every industry, or leave it.

One of Jack Welch's most "celebrated" management techniques was to fire the bottom 10 percent of his managers every year and reward the top 20 percent with bonuses and stock options. He was candid and fearless, and he never wavered from his principles.

While this management style was controversial (he was known as "Neutron Jack"), it was a huge value driver. When Welch became CEO, revenues were about $27 billion. When he left they were nearly $130 billion.

Upon retirement, Welch's brand kept growing in strength and influence. He became a celebrity author and speaker, commanding fees for his appearances as large as a former president of the United States. You might say his already formidable leader brand went platinum. Everyone wanted to learn something from the man who made GE the largest company in the world.

Some of the defining aspects of the Welch brand are a focus on winning, ruthless decisiveness, and brazen candor. People admire these qualities. They want to understand them. They want to emulate him. They appreciate how powerful his brand is, and how these values shaped and determined GE's success.

MARK ZUCKERBERG, FACEBOOK

Mark Zuckerberg, founder and CEO of Facebook, has exploded onto the business scene. He's the new kid on the brand block. By his mid-twenties, Zuckerberg was already leading a blockbuster company. Facebook's technology platform, driven by an underlying philosophy we'll examine shortly, was profoundly influencing our culture.

What is the Zuckerberg brand, and how has it shaped Facebook? Like Jack Welch, Zuckerberg has a philosophy, shaped by experiences and values formed at a young age. As a Harvard student, with the help of a few friends, he launched a technology platform where students could share personal information with one another. The underpinning of it all was a game-changing concept: the rejection of the modern notion of privacy. He didn't embrace privacy the way past generations like baby boomers had. He believed in sharing personal information digitally. This was in sync with the philosophy of his generation, to open up and share. Transparency was his brand. It became the brand of Facebook.

The brand is authentic. Zuckerberg actually lives a transparent life. For example, in 2010, his Facebook friends still had access to his e-mail and his cell phone. They could check out his personal photos from backyard parties, even though he was a celebrity. His company was valued in the billions, and yet he still posted his whereabouts through Facebook's feature "Places." An article in *New Yorker* magazine in September 2010 documented that at 2:45 a.m., Eastern Standard Time, on August 29, he was at the Ace Hotel, in New York City's garment district. He was back at Facebook's headquarters, in Palo Alto, California, by 7:08 p.m., Pacific Standard Time. On August 31 at 10:38 p.m., he and his girlfriend were eating dinner at Taqueria La Bamba, in Mountain View, California.

In his Facebook bio, Zuckerberg explains, "I'm trying to make the world a more open place." This personal philosophy is the underlying brand driver that has catapulted Facebook from a dorm room start-up to the biggest social network in the world. His brand and the company brand are one. And it is worth billions.

Your brand is different from all other brands. You bring something unique, exciting, and powerful to the enterprise you lead.

Ironically, Zuckerberg seems uncomfortable in the limelight. The opposite of a Jack Welch, who embraced his celebrity, Zuckerberg approaches television appearances and print interviews awkwardly. It is interesting that even though *transparency* is his brand, it doesn't translate to being *outgoing*. He seems to want to retreat behind a veil of an electronic persona. And, that's utterly consistent with the Facebook brand and the users it attracts. The brand is all about digital intimacy.

SO WHAT DO THESE TWO BRANDS HAVE TO DO WITH *YOUR* BRAND?

These are just two examples of leaders whose brands have shaped the brands and created value in their companies. Like them, you have a unique brand, different from all others. You bring something singular and powerful to the enterprise you lead. This is true whether you are the founder or the leader running the organization today. This is why it is so important to truly understand and embrace your brand. It becomes the fulcrum for creating value.

Whether you are the CEO, or the leader of a team, division, committee, or nonprofit organization, you have a brand. There is a power and dynamic to your brand. And if you want to be a leader someday, now is the time to start thinking about your brand. As you go forward in your career, become mindful of the events that shape you. This will help you define yourself as a leader. You'll be able to communicate your brand in ways that make an impact on the organization you lead.

It is amazing how you can transform an organization when you know and understand your own brand. I once coached the CIO of the largest division of a major financial services firm. This leader was widely admired and well known for his brand values. I worked with his entire team, so I can tell you, based on personal interviews and experience, that *every single one of his direct reports, every one of their direct reports, and people the next layer down,* could tell you the three words that were important to their success—three words that happened to define this leader's brand; courage, candor, and integrity. He lived his brand, talked about these values, and by words and example, encouraged others to live them. Not surprisingly, his team vastly outperformed all others in that function across the company.

Why was he so successful? At first, he focused on communicating the brand value to his own team. They soon were able to act on those values. After a while, they became very good at communicating them as well. As a high-performing team, they constantly referred to these values, and they also talked about how much they admired the leader. His team knew what he stood for, respected him, and saw the power of those ideas and values in making them successful. They adopted his way and measured themselves against it. But it all began because he knew himself, knew what he stood for, and knew how to communicate that to others.

As a leader you can do the same thing for your organization. As already mentioned, this advice isn't just for CEOs, although it is a critical factor for chief executives. Anyone who leads should start today, to examine his or her brand values. The more clarity you have, the more powerful the results you can achieve for your organization. I can't emphasize this point enough. With a powerful brand you become an influential force, a touchstone for others, shaping and influencing the culture and character of an organization. Your brand can actually alter the very DNA of the company, organization, or team you serve.

BRAND ALIGNMENT

As you might imagine you won't be successful if your brand values and the company's are in direct conflict. There has to be alignment between your values, and those of the organization. Every leader must assess the connection between her or his brand and the company brand. When your brand and the company brand are out of sync, you are not in a role that suits you.

All you have to do is read the *Wall Street Journal* on any given day to find examples of leaders and companies whose brands are out of sync. If a leader's brand becomes tarnished or toxic, it hurts the company, and the leader and company inevitably part ways, often after a public battle. Conversely, when a company's brand is toxic, the CEO or leader must exert influence to reignite the brand. If the leader has a strong brand and is influential, his or her brand can revive and replenish the company brand.

When there is alignment—when the leader's brand and the company brand are in sync—there is tremendous harmony in the organization. This harmony drives real, tangible value. Why? Your brand attracts people to you. It generates amazing energy. When people resonate with your brand, and see it living in the organization, they want to work for you. You attract high quality employees and leaders who are loyal to you. Investors, shareholders, customers, and vendors also want to do business with you. People recognize and feel the energy when a leader and the organization are in sync, generating positive energy.

BRAND IMAGE

When you think of great company brands, they make a strong impression. The associations are logical and emotional. If I show you a picture of a suite in the Ritz-Carlton hotel, a Harley-Davidson motorcycle racing down the road, a frosty glass of Budweiser beer, or a Mercedes-Benz parked in a grand circular driveway, you have an instant thought that evokes a feeling. You may, with little effort, think of three words that sum up each of those brands.

Now, think about your favorite boss—someone you admire—someone who was influential in your life. Jot down three words that you think define him or her. It isn't difficult, is it? Those three words summarize a multitude of experiences you have had with that person, which have formed and reinforced impressions.

This doesn't imply that anyone can sum you up in three words. You are a lot more than that—but when people know your brand they can quickly describe you in a few words. Our brains are programmed to build circuits to words and feelings that help us remember and describe people.

A BRAND IN THREE WORDS

Harley-Davidson

1. Speed

2. Freedom

3. Community

New York Jets

1. Braggers

2. Tough guys

3. Ultra-confident

Richard Branson

1. Daring

2. Risk taker

3. Adventurer

A Leader You've Known (Three Words)

Name _____

1. _____

2. _____

3. _____

You may not know what three words describe you, but as you read this book you will get clarity. The goal of the book isn't to be able to sum up your leadership in three words, but rather to help you understand how authentic brand impressions are formed about leaders. As you get clear about this, you can communicate who you are in a way that drives value.

Brands are not first impressions. A brand is built over time. The words describe a relationship people have with you based on many observations or experiences. The brand words are a product of events that form impressions that live on in other's minds.

That's why it is important to understand yourself and be able to communicate your brand. Just like Jack Welch or Mark Zuckerberg, over time your brand will become known, and it will make a big impact on your organization. People will watch you, listen to you, and anchor what they know into a brand impression.

WHAT MAKES YOUR BRAND VALUABLE?

When it comes to great companies, there's no question that brand value is a tangible asset. For example, according to the *BrandZ Top 100 Report* (Millward-Brown, in conjunction with the *Financial Times*, *Bloomberg*, and Datamonitor), the most valuable brand in 2010 was Google. The ranking is based on company valuation as well as positive consumer feedback, from survey data, product sales, top-line growth, and/or bottom-line profit. In other words, Google's value goes beyond its assets and even its balance sheet. A significant part of Google's value is the impression people have formed based on their experience with it. There is intrinsic value in Google's name and reputation that transcends the tangible assets.

Similarly, there is intrinsic value in your name and reputation. How do you *measure* the value of your *own* brand? It may be easier to answer that question by reverse engineering and reviewing a famous example of a brand disaster. Sadly, some leaders and celebrities are best known for throwing away their stellar brands.

Tiger Woods did tremendous damage to his reputation in the scandal around his personal life, and it cost him dearly. Woods wasn't just on his way to becoming the best *golfer* of all time; he was also the wealthiest, best-known *athlete* in the *world*. The scandal cost him not only tournament winnings but also $35 million in endorsements from companies, including Accenture and Procter & Gamble. Beyond those losses, the future value of his brand would never be the same, even if he came back and played like the champion he was in previous years. Chapter 9 examines more closely other brand disasters and what we can learn from them.

But back to the main issue—the value of your brand. It's only logical that your brand adds value, in real dollars and in so many other ways. GE would have been a successful company under any leader, but it was *wildly* successful under Jack Welch. The intrinsic value of the Jack Welch brand added great value. Who he was and what he stood for lived in the very fabric of GE, and that dramatically drove up revenue and shareholder value.

WHAT'S THE CURRENT AND FUTURE VALUE OF *YOUR* BRAND?

When marketing experts talk about brand equity, they are referring to a set of attributes that include brand awareness, perceived quality, brand loyalty, and other associations such as people who endorse it. These attributes all create value.

Brand attributes can accrue to a company or product, and brand value can also be accrued to a leader who commands a high level of respect and influence in his or her company or industry. When people know you, believe you represent certain qualities, and resonate with those qualities or attributes, the value of your brand is high. You attract great employees, new clients, opportunities, business partnerships, referral relationships, endorsements, testimonials, and networks of leaders, all of which you will be able to trace to revenue and profitability. The better people know and respect your brand, the more they understand it and feel alignment with it, the more these valuable relationships and profitable opportunities come along. Your brand value grows.

So, the present value of your brand is measured today by how well people know you and how much they value your brand; the future value of your brand will be determined by how much more clearly you define that brand and communicate it to others. That's why it is so important to do the exciting, challenging, and rewarding work of the next few chapters. You'll find the "platinum" that is your brand and how to communicate that to raise your profile and leverage your brand equity.

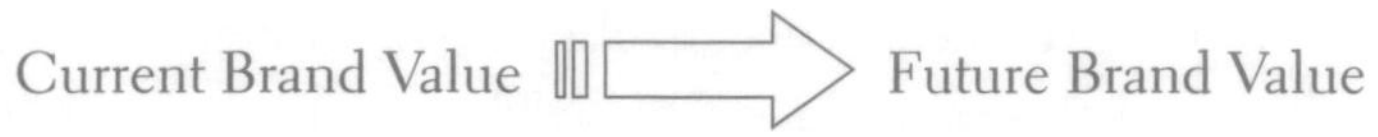

Current Brand Value ▯▯ ⟹ Future Brand Value

*To increase current brand value, understand it
and communicate it effectively.*

Figure 1.1

It stands to reason that just being clear about your brand values isn't enough; people need to know who you are and what you stand for. That's why communicating your leadership brand, so it is recognized in a variety of forums, will make your brand potent. High awareness of your brand, and a perception of your value to the organization, makes you a powerful leader, and builds brand equity. The better you communicate your brand, the wider your circle of influence, the greater asset your brand becomes. See Figure 1.1.

> The present value of your brand is what it is; the future value is what you will make it.

The way to build a great leader brand is to understand the values and principles that have shaped you and made you who you are as a leader, then to communicate this to a wider and wider group of important audiences. Your current brand value will grow as you understand it and learn to communicate it effectively

As you read the next few chapters, be open to examining your brand, and as you get clear about that, you'll find it easy to communicate and amplify your brand with employees, customers, partners, investors, the media, and the public.

LEVERAGING THE FUTURE VALUE OF YOUR BRAND

There are countless ways to leverage the future value of your brand— as many ways as there are leaders. Just remember, above all, it has to be authentic to you. An authentic brand is essential. Authenticity builds trust. People know when your brand is real. You don't have to be perfect. Real isn't perfect. Real is real. Your brand is most powerful when you communicate what is true about you.

A trusted authentic brand has sticking power—or what is called "brand loyalty." Loyalty exists when people understand your brand, and trust it. In the world of products and services, loyalty is the commitment to repurchase or keep using the brand. When it comes to leaders, it's commitment to stay with the leader through thick and thin. People believe in you.

Brand loyalty drives even greater value; loyalty increases the number of talented people you attract and retain, the number of customers who do business with you year after year, the number of investors who go multiple rounds funding you, and the number of referrals you get from customers who talk you up. Brand loyalty generates more positive media attention that builds your company's reputation.

> To leverage your brand it has to have sticking power—or what is called "brand loyalty."

The more you learn about leveraging your brand, the more you can create value. You'll be able to build a brand that can get you booked to speak at major conferences where you meet new customers. You will get invitations to join networks or organizations you didn't have access to before. You will interact with other influential industry leaders, policy makers, political leaders, joint venture partners, investors, and more.

You will also find that a trusted brand is a buffer for your company in challenging times. You get the benefit of the doubt. You can step in and change the conversation. You can cushion the blow. You can pave the way for a better outcome. A respected brand will help you win back another's trust. Of course, you already have to have the brand to use it in times of crisis. When a crisis hits, it's too late to build a trusted brand.

As you learn to leverage your leader brand, you will see what value it has. You will begin to notice a direct impact on the success of your company. You may not always know what is working but if you are living and communicating your brand every day, you will see tangible results. There's an old saying in marketing: "50 percent of my marketing is working; I'm just not sure which 50 percent." When you live your brand, the same dynamic is in play. In the next chapter, we'll look at lessons from leaders who have built exceptional brands.

CHAPTER SUMMARY

- Your leader brand is one of the most powerful tools you have.
- You can leverage your unique, personal brand to drive value into your company.
- There are as many brands as there are leaders.
- This book will help you uncover your authentic leadership brand.
- You'll discover how your life and career story have shaped your brand.
- You'll be inspired by the stories of leaders who have built great brands.
- And you'll find practical tools for communicating your brand to the world.
- The tools and exercises in this book are practical and apply to anyone who wants to lead.

How Exceptional Leader Brands Are Built

A brand for a company is like a reputation for a person.
You earn reputation by trying to do hard things well.

—Jeff Bezos, CEO, Amazon

WHAT CAN WE LEARN FROM LEADERS who have built exceptional brands? In this chapter I've chosen to explore a few "household names"—modern-day leaders and celebrities who have become the "Mercedes-Benz" of their industries. They define their categories. They are standouts among standouts. We know their histories, but what do those stories tell us about how to build a brand?

You don't have to be Richard Branson, Warren Buffett, Bill Gates, or Oprah Winfrey to be standout leader in your own category. The point of sharing these stories is to show you how their stories shape their brands. The idea is not to become like them, but to learn by analyzing the way their personal brands became so valuable. How did they create and accelerate the brand value, equity, and loyalty that we discussed in the previous chapter? How did they go from nowhere to somewhere to everywhere?

As you read their stories, keep in mind that I'm not suggesting that you emulate these people, but be inspired by how they went about doing what they did. Read about the events that shaped them and defined them, and as you do so, ask yourself, "What's *my* story?" Let their stories inspire you and prepare you for Chapter 3, when we start exploring and analyzing the story of *you*.

RICHARD BRANSON, VIRGIN GROUP

The biggest and boldest business and CEO brand today arguably belongs to Sir Richard Charles Nicholas Branson, the daring, adventurous British industrialist who presides over Virgin Group. His business empire encompasses 400 companies. His reputation is global. From Virgin Atlantic Airways to Virgin Mobile, Virgin Blue, Virgin Trains, Virgin America, and Virgin Vodka (one of the few brands that hasn't been a success), Branson has made his mark. He is known for setting audacious goals and building hugely successful enterprises. He has an astounding imagination and mind-blowing courage. One of his most amazing and creative ventures: the space tourism company, Virgin Galactic, whose mission is to take civilian passengers into suborbital space.

Branson isn't just a business magnate; he's a swashbuckling adventurer. He has attempted dangerous ocean crossings and crossed continents in a hot-air balloon. He's gone global on humanitarian efforts, becoming a financial backer for a group of world thought leaders, led by Nelson Mandela, whose charter is to solve conflicts and foster world peace.

Branson's passion, gusto, and zeal for life are boundless. What makes his story all the more compelling is that he was born in a nursing home for children with special needs, has severe dyslexia, and had always struggled in school. He started humbly, selling cutout albums from the back of his car—a small venture that morphed into his first successful business, Virgin Records. The Virgin name, by the way, was a reference to how he and a few first employees considered themselves virgins in business. Boy, have they come a long way!

RICHARD BRANSON'S BRAND

Be Fearless

If I asked you to select three words to describe Branson's brand, you'd have to narrow it down from a long list, but perhaps you'd offer *trailblazer*, *explorer*, and *buccaneer*. In his autobiography, Branson said, "My interest in life comes from setting myself huge, apparently unachievable challenges and trying to rise above them . . . from the perspective of wanting to live life to the full, I felt that I had to attempt it." Branson has made his mark by going big, then going bigger, and then imagining how much bigger he could go.

Branson's brand is fearlessness. This brand attracts people who drive the vision and help him create enormously successful enterprises. His quest for adventure has become his calling card. You might say the essence of it is, "Be fearless."

SHAQUILLE O'NEAL, NBA STAR

No, he isn't a CEO, but Shaquille "Shaq" O'Neal is a very big man, with a very big personality, who presides over a very big and impressive personal business empire. While Shaq's imposing frame gives him a distinct advantage on the basketball court, his brand is far more than his seven-foot, one-inch frame. After all, there's no shortage of tall guys in the National Basketball Association (NBA). Shaq is larger than life. His personality shines. That's why those size 23 shoes have left a big footprint in entertainment. His playful attitude and brilliant rapport with the press and the public have made him a star far beyond the NBA.

An indication of his popularity and connection are his nicknames. He has more than any professional athlete, including The Diesel, Shaq Fu, The Big Aristotle, The Big Daddy, Superman, The Big Cactus, The Big Shaqtus, The Big Galactus, Wilt Chamberneezy, The Big Baryshnikov, The Real Deal, Dr. Shaq (after earning his MBA), The Big Shamrock (after he joined the Celtics), The Big Leprechaun, Shaquovic, and (after conducting the Boston Pops 2010 Holiday Concert) The Big Conductor. He's played for the Magic, the Lakers, the Heat, the Suns, the Cavaliers, and the Celtics.

Shaq's screen credits look like Santa's Christmas list, far too numerous to mention. He's appeared everywhere from *Curb Your Enthusiasm* to

Saturday Night Live and his own reality show in 2007. He's released five rap music albums, and he's been praised for his musical talent. He performs in music videos, and does voice-overs in animated films. He's acted in feature film roles. He shows up on video games and documentary films from ABC to ESPN to Discovery.

Shaq is beloved and utterly believable. It's not an act. He's really having fun. He's a serious competitor who doesn't take the pressure of being "Shaq" too seriously. He enjoys the limelight. He doesn't just sign autographs. He has a blast being Shaq.

SHAQUILLE O'NEAL'S BRAND

Have Fun Being You

In essence, the brand "message" from Shaq's life and career? "Have fun being you."

WARREN BUFFETT, BERKSHIRE HATHAWAY

Warren Buffett—yes, he's rich. Yes, he's powerful. Yes he seems to have cornered the secrets of success in business. Everything he touches turns to gold. But what can he teach us? Isn't he a brand just because he's at the top of *Fortune*'s list of the world's wealthiest people, year after year? Actually, no!

In 2010, Buffett wasn't actually number one. That honor went to Mexico's Carlos Slim. Who? I'm not saying no one knows who he is, but he's not exactly a household name, especially in the United States. Neither are Mukesh Ambani or Lakshmi Mittal, who are right behind Buffett in net worth, or Bernard Arnault, Eike Batista, and Amancio Ortega, who are right behind them. Again, you're probably asking, "Who?"

The point is that Buffett's global name brand is more than his money. His brand is the knowledge he shares. Even the average Joe knows something about how Buffett makes money! How do we know? He tells us! Unlike other wealthy, successful businesspeople, he has made it a practice to share his wealth-building secrets. And you can trace this back to his childhood and early career.

Growing up, Buffett was an industrious kid, making and saving money. He went door to door selling chewing gum and weekly magazines. He worked in his grandfather's store, delivered newspapers, sold golf balls and stamps, and detailed cars. He was—and is—famously frugal. On his first tax return in 1944, he took a $35 deduction for the bike he used on his paper route. He still lives in the same house in Omaha that he bought in 1958 for $31,500, though he also owns a multimillion-dollar home in California.

As he learned about making money, he wanted to tell other people about how to do it. As a stockbroker, he took a Dale Carnegie course in public speaking, and he decided to teach an Investment Principles night class at the University of Nebraska, Omaha. Today his philosophy—buy quality and hold long term to build wealth—is his mantra, known the world over. By purchasing private companies and taking investment positions in public ones, he has demonstrated how his principles work. Many books document his wealth principles, from *The Warren Buffett Way* to *How to Pick Stocks Like Warren Buffett*.

Buffett's brand has become even more potent as he has announced that, upon his death, 99 percent of his wealth will be given away, and as he has launched a campaign to get other megarich people to give theirs away, too. In 2011, when a man considered to be his successor, David L. Sokol, came under investigation for potential S.E.C. violations, it threatened to ding Buffett's brand. But the strength of his reputation also appeared to be insulating him from permanent brand damage. The essence of his brand remained, "share the wisdom."

WARREN BUFFETT'S BRAND

Share Your Wisdom

BILL GATES, THE BILL AND MELINDA GATES FOUNDATION

While on the subject of wildly wealthy businesspeople, we can hardly ignore one of Buffett's closest friends, Microsoft founder Bill Gates. Gates's story also is well documented—he is the best known of the group of 1970s entrepreneurs who led the personal computer revolution. Admired by many, perhaps despised by some, for the anticompetitive practices Microsoft championed, Gates has now stepped away from Microsoft's day-to-day operations to become a philanthropist.

Gates and his wife, Melinda, launched the Bill and Melinda Gates Foundation in 2000, now said to be the largest transparently operated private foundation in the world. Their projects focus on reducing poverty and improving health care around the world, as well as expanding opportunities for education and access to technology. It has an endowment of more than $30 billion.

The foundation is making an impact globally, in places where vaccines and immunizations are needed for AIDS, tuberculosis, and malaria. It researches how to grow rice to end starvation, makes grants to earthquake victims, builds schools, gives scholarships, and donates computers to libraries. In this, and in his enormously successful business enterprise, Bill Gates's brand has become about one thing: having an impact.

Many wealthy people give money away. Gates wanted to give it away with purpose. Once he realized that people expected him to be philanthropic, he studied the work of Andrew Carnegie and John D. Rockefeller. He decided to have a focus—to address global issues poorly managed by governments.

One of the hallmarks of strongly branded leaders is that they are well known for something because they focus on that one thing like a laser. Early on, Gates focused on what the world needed going forward—computers—and he built the most powerful software platforms on the planet; later he focused on making an impact on another problem at the "planetary level," helping poor and underprivileged people achieve health.

BILL GATES'S BRAND

Focus and Make an Impact

It is a challenge for every leader to focus when we have so many distractions and possibilities; however, if you look at extraordinary leaders like Gates, they focus like a laser where they can make a big impact.

DIANE VON FURSTENBERG, FASHION DESIGNER

Her biography reads like a novel; her iconic knitted jersey "wrap dress," first introduced in 1973, is now in the collection of the Costume Institute of the Metropolitan Museum of Art. She owned the title of princess when, at the University of Geneva, she met and married Prince Egon von Furstenberg. In the 1970s, after a separation from the prince, she was known for her breezy glamour and jet-set lifestyle. Her figure-hugging fashion swept the Studio 54 and Park Avenue crowd. Many years later she gave up the single life and agreed to marry longtime companion and media mogul Barry Diller as a birthday present.

The wrap is a dress with two front panels that wrap across each other and tie; almost like wearing a sexy bathrobe to the office or a party. In the 2000s, an entirely new generation discovered the wrap, and von Furstenberg's company soared again. She expanded into new business lines, such as cosmetics and home shopping. It was a testament to the timelessness of her fashion and her *personal* brand.

Von Furstenberg is all about celebrating the beauty and strength of women. Having started her company in 1970 with a $30,000 investment, she believed in independence. She has always exuded her brand. *Town & Country* magazine once referred to it as "the sultriness of a biblical temptress." She displays a natural confidence and easy-flowing style. One of the few famous women her age (in their sixties) who eschews Botox, von Furstenberg also appears fearless about getting older.

Another defining characteristic of her brand is her outspoken leadership in the fashion industry. Never afraid of stirring up a little trouble, she publicly rejects the size-zero model phenomenon that has dominated the industry, and chides her fashion industry colleagues to promote healthier images of women as well as diversity in culture. As president of the Council of Fashion Designers of America (CFDA), she once sent a memo to members encouraging them to make their fashion shows "truly multicultural," and she has more black models than most designers.

DIANE VON FURSTENBERG'S BRAND

Live Your Brand

Von Furstenberg epitomizes that person who truly, deeply lives her brand. The creation of her brand comes from the inside. She embodies the brand and models it for the world to see. And that is what great leaders with powerful brands do—they live their brands. As you read ahead, and think about your own brand, ask yourself not just what is my brand, but how do I live my brand, every day?

CONDOLEEZZA RICE, DIPLOMAT, ACADEMIC, MUSICIAN

In 2010, *Time* magazine named Condoleezza Rice among the 100 people who are most influencing the world. When asked about the greatest learning moment of her life, she told the magazine that it was her effort to become a competitive figure skater. "I learned how to work very hard at something, not successfully, and still get up and keep trying," she says. "For me that was more important than doing things that I did well."

As most people know, Rice was a figure in the George H. W. Bush administration. After a stint back at Stanford University, she became the first woman national security advisor under President George W. Bush, and then, the second woman secretary of state after Madeleine Albright.

Known as a strong and thoughtful leader, Rice pioneered a policy called "transformational diplomacy" that emphasized getting democratically elected governments in place in troubled parts of the world.

Her path to international prominence is a story of hard work and tremendous discipline. Growing up in racially divided Birmingham, Alabama, she lived in a place where blacks were told to keep their heads down or face the consequences. Her first ambition had been to be a concert pianist, but sensing she didn't have the talent to take it all the way, Rice studied political science, eventually earning a Ph.D. with a dissertation on military policy and politics in then Czechoslovakia. She rose through the ranks of Stanford University from tenured professor to provost, second in command, and was appointed director on numerous corporate boards.

In her autobiography, *Extraordinary, Ordinary People*, Rice shared that her parents were "convinced that education was a kind of armor shielding me against everything, even the deep racism in Birmingham and across America." Rice said, "There was nothing worse than being a helpless victim of your circumstances. Needless to say [my parents] were even more determined that I not end up that way."

With all these accomplishments, what is the thread that defines her brand? It's the work ethic. As Jeff Bezos of Amazon says, "You earn a reputation by trying to do hard things well." Though Rice never played piano professionally, she debuted as a pianist with the Denver Symphony at age 15 and has continued to play the instrument all her life. That prompted the *New York Times* to name her the world's foremost amateur musician.

CONDOLEEZZA RICE'S BRAND

Do the Hard Things Well

Rice's commitment to excellence is a signature piece of her exceptional brand.

ANNE MULCAHY, FORMER CEO, XEROX CORPORATION

Shortly after Anne Mulcahy was thrust to the helm at Xerox in 2000, with the company facing possible bankruptcy, her message to shareholders was, "Xerox's business model is unsustainable." The board had just fired CEO Richard Thoman, after 13 months on the job. The day after Mulcahy's appointment Xerox stock dropped 26 percent.

While Mulcahy might have been more diplomatic, that was never her style. Equal parts warm and engaging, and also blunt and courageous, she told the top 100 leaders now was the time to leave with a healthy financial package, or sign on and commit. Only three left.

Having been at Xerox 25 years, and held a variety of positions from sales and marketing to human resources, she knew the people and the culture and believed in the Xerox values. The financial team urged her to declare bankruptcy. She refused. Warren Buffet told her to avoid the bankers and spend all your time with customers and employees. That's precisely what she did.

Xerox went from losing $300 million annually when Mulcahy took over in 2000, to a $1 billion profit in a few short years. Through cost cutting, including the elimination of 28,000 jobs, she maneuvered through the near-death experience and then put Xerox on a path to transformation through technology and innovation. Her vision had been realized by the time she handed over the reins in a well-planned succession, that had two years earlier identified Ursula Burns as the next CEO.

ANN MULCAHY'S BRAND

Loyalty and Faith

In a speech to The Commonwealth Institute in Boston in 2011, she told a crowd of women leaders how truly stressful the times were. Yet today she and those who weathered the storm and brought Xerox back to profitability regard it as the most exciting time in their careers.

Once when an angry customer told her she needed to kill the Xerox culture, she shot back, "I am the culture." Today as Chair of Save the Children she now pours her passion into a new cause. But her role in bringing back an iconic brand from the brink of ruin has burnished her brand: loyalty to Xerox and faith in its people.

BONO, ROCK STAR AND PHILANTHROPIST

As the lead singer of U2, one of the most popular and influential rock bands of the last 30 years, Bono is perhaps another unlikely choice for a book on CEO brands. But Bono has carved out a leadership position far beyond rock and roll. He's become a global force inside and outside the music industry for his work in humanitarian causes.

Where did he come by this authentic desire to make a difference in the world? Growing up in deeply sectarian Ireland as the son of a Catholic father and a Protestant mother, Bono's upbringing was unusual and traumatic. When Bono was 14, his mother died of a brain hemorrhage at the funeral of her own father, and subsequently, Bono says, he and his father fought and never really reconciled. Bono claimed his father's unspoken message was that "to dream is to be disappointed," and in rebellion, the son grew determined to do something big with his life.

If there's a word that fans and admirers might use to describe Bono, it might be *connection*. On stage, Bono has walked out on tables, kissed the girls, and drunk their wine; it has become his signature, even at Live Aid in 1985. Detractors have sometimes derided the Messiah-like atmosphere, but there's no doubt that he has been a force of one.

As his influence has grown, he has become passionate about his activist causes. He started by going to Ethiopia to work with his wife, Ali, at a food camp. He later championed causes from Amnesty International to Greenpeace, campaigning against AIDS, and launching his own non-governmental organizations (NGOs), such as DATA (Debt, Aid, Trade Africa) and the ONE Campaign to Make Poverty History. He once said, "The world is more malleable than you think, and it's waiting for you to hammer it into shape."

BONO'S BRAND

The Power of One

What you see in people with such enormous influence is epitomized in Bono's brand—it's a belief in the "power of one." Leaders with powerful brands make a point to reach out and touch others. They typically are not cynical; rather, they believe they have an opportunity to influence, and they do so. Bono claimed that power of one, and believes in his own ability to influence.

FRED SMITH, CHAIRMAN, PRESIDENT, CEO, FEDEX

Legend has it that Fred Smith first broached the idea for express delivery in 1965 while an economics major at Yale. Though he doesn't remember the grade, the professor is said to have told him that the idea would be worth a C, if it were viable. Born in 1944 in Marks, Mississippi, Smith had transportation in his DNA—from the grandfather who was a steamboat captain, to the father who built a regional bus line from the ground up and sold it to become the southern backbone of the Greyhound Bus System.

Smith served four years in the Marines, from 1966 to 1969, where he had the chance to study precision military logistics as a platoon leader and FAC (Forward Air Controller). Specially trained to fly with pilots, he earned a Bronze Star, Silver Star, and two Purple Hearts. And all the while he was fine-tuning his idea for an overnight delivery service, which he modeled on the same idea as a central bank clearing house.

With a $4 million inheritance and another $91 in investment capital he launched Federal Express in 1971 with the promise of overnight delivery of critical goods between any two points in an 11-city network he created. It was hardly an overnight success. His first run was seven packages; the postal monopoly kept him from expanding from packages to documents into the 1970s; he was once so strapped for cash he flew to Las Vegas to play Blackjack. But FedEx wasn't just the first; it became and remained the leader in the just-in-time delivery marketplace, known for its commitment to total quality service. As a $39 billion global transportation and logistics business, it has operations in 220 countries, handles 8.5 million shipments each business day, and has been recognized among *Fortune's* Most Admired Companies and Best Companies to Work For. He has been a winner of *Chief Executive* magazine's CEO of the year.

There's no question that Fred Smith epitomized the can-do American—he had an idea and never stopped believing, never stopped driving, until it became one of the most iconic business brands in the world. His conviction and commitment to quality became the heart of the FedEx brand, driving enormous value into the business. Smith made a cameo appearance as himself in the movie *Castaway* when Tom Hanks's character is welcomed back at the actual FedEx headquarters in Memphis, Tennessee; he has friends in politics from John Kerry to George Bush, a classmate and DKE fraternity brother at Yale. He was twice rumored to be a candidate for U.S. Secretary of Defense. But it is his commitment to an idea that is the heart of the Fred Smith brand, one that made him one of the most admired CEOs of his time.

FRED SMITH BRAND

Total Commitment to Success

CHAPTER SUMMARY

- You can learn much from the people who have built mega-brands.
- Every leader's brand is unique and based on his or her story.
- Leaders who have strong brands apply the principles mentioned in this chapter.
- The essence of your brand is the story of you.

3

Your CEO Brand—The Story of You

The essence of American presidential leadership, and the secret of presidential success, is storytelling.

—Evan Cornog, *The Power and the Story: How the Crafted Presidential Narrative Has Determined Political Success from George Washington to George W. Bush*

IT'S TIME NOW TO DISCOVER YOUR story—the story of your brand. In this chapter we will explore the events, challenges, obstacles, and experiences have shaped you. You will learn how to explore these stories and tell them in a way that defines you as a leader. You're about to discover a step-by-step process for uncovering the story of you.

If you've never looked at the stories of your life and career, you're going to enjoy it. This process will help you to clarify and refine the lessons that have shaped your brand. You will go to a deeper level to learn what you're all about as a leader.

This is a very important step in the process of building your brand, so I urge you to actually stop and answer the questions. It's tempting to read on, or skip to the next chapter and tell yourself that you'll go back and do it later. I encourage you to stop, think, write, and learn about yourself. You will find that looking at these events in your life in an entirely new way is not only deeply rewarding but also fun.

Some of the stories you remember may be ones you've told in the past. You already may have a sense of how they have shaped you as a leader. You may also have had the experience of seeing the impact stories have on an audience. If you've never done so, you're about to discover the power of the story in communicating your brand.

Over the years, in working with leaders, I've found that many haven't taken the time to examine the stories of their lives and career. Often that means they aren't really sure what they are all about as leaders. They know how to run a business but they haven't taken the time to examine their lives and careers, and define who they are as leaders. By embracing this process, you will be able to see your life experiences in a new way. This will enable you to take charge of your brand and communicate what you want others to know about you.

WHAT IS THE CONNECTION BETWEEN PERSONALITY AND BRAND?

Before we move forward, one aspect of brand that people often talk about is your personality. Personality is one *element* of your brand—but it is not the sum total. For example, you may be outgoing, funny, analytical, thoughtful, or unconventional. Those are interesting qualities about you, but they don't provide a complete picture of your brand. The complete picture of your brand is based on the values and principles that define you. That's what we can learn from your stories.

Your brand also is much more than executive presence, such as the clothes you wear, the way you carry yourself, and so on. Those elements of executive presence are symbols of your ability to fit into a leadership role, but they only reflect your brand. Your brand is defined by the personal values you hold, formed through the lessons you have learned from your experiences, and how you communicate it through words and actions.

> The core of your brand is what's inside—the ideas, principles, and values that you live by.

The core of your brand is what's inside your character and values—and those become clear through your stories. That is why storytelling is so important to leadership. So, it's time to find those signature stories that communicate your brand.

As you go through the process, don't hesitate to recall stories even if you are not sure what they have to do with your brand. Don't reject the story too early in the process, until you've examined the details of the experience. Your stories are your stories, what make you the person you are. Enter into the process without preconceived ideas about what you're going to learn about yourself. Let the stories tell you what they are going to tell you about you.

The outcome of this process will be a guide to understanding your leadership brand. No one else but you can interpret your story the way you can, although you will probably find it valuable to identify a partner, friend, or coach to help you.

Your journey to understanding your brand begins with a question that we all want to know the answer to: who are you?

WHO ARE YOU?

Back in the 1970s the English rock band The Who (lead singer Roger Daltrey, guitarist and songwriter Pete Townshend, bassist John Entwistle, and drummer Keith Moon) recorded one of the anthems of the generation, "Who Are You?" In the song, a chorus poses this haunting rhetorical question: "Who are you? Who, who, who, who?"

Okay, the song is about a guy who wakes up in Soho after a drunken, brawling night, and the band wasn't thinking about CEOs and leaders. But those words still ring in our ears beyond the hangover of our youth. The older we get, the more we think about who we are and what we're all about. Figuring out what your life is all about is part of understanding your brand.

So let's get started.

Read the following story, about a leader who has built a brand, with an eye toward analyzing how you think his brand developed. Look for clues as to what shaped him and how he translated that into leadership principles, the key to his business success.

DAVID PISOR, ELYSIAN HOTELS

David Pisor, the managing principal and CEO of a luxury hotel and residence in Chicago, has a unique and refreshing approach to his business. He is the innovator and brains behind Elysian, a unique, high-end property in the heart of Chicago's Gold Coast. Pisor's dream was to reimagine ultra-luxury living. Elysian has a sophisticated and timeless Art Deco–inspired setting, with 188 guest rooms and 52 private residences that sell for millions of dollars. The property has two extraordinary restaurants, as well as a bar, health club, and spa. It's drop-dead glamorous. But glamour isn't the essence of the brand.

Pisor grew up, not with a silver spoon in his mouth, but in a middle-class home inside the city limits of Detroit. He went to public schools. His family was comfortable but not wealthy. His father was a news reporter for the NBC television station in Detroit. They moved into the city when David's father was appointed press secretary for Mayor Coleman Young. They were required to have residency in what was at that time one of America's most depressed and volatile cities.

Pisor became adept at tuning into others. "I learned how to read people very well." He worked many jobs including bus boy at the Detroit Golf Club, which gave him the "means" to go to concerts or travel.

After college, Pisor made his way to California, where he got his first taste of high-end hospitality at Chez Panisse, a San Francisco restaurant founded by the influential and visionary chef Alice Waters, his aunt. "She had an incredible influence on me. What I learned about from her was quality," says Pisor. "She insisted on the very best food, grown in the best conditions, and prepared in the best ways," he said.

> "She [Alice Waters] had an incredible influence on me. What I learned about from her was quality," says Pisor.

Pisor came back to the Midwest, got into commercial real estate, started a technology company, sold it at the height of the 1990s boom, and then had the freedom to do something he was passionate about—building a luxury hotel and residence. They broke ground in Chicago in 2004.

What's the brand? Pisor would say it's his "take" on what luxury really is—an intimate experience, not the usual canned, scripted, formal, or by-the-book approach. Guests don't have to check in; they are met at the airport or greeted at the door as if they were coming home. No standing in line at the desk. Remember all those years that Pisor spent learning how to read people? And the importance he places on humility? Well, that's part of the Elysian brand. Employees are taught to "read" their guests. They don't assume you want to be called "Mr. Jones;" they ask what you want to be called, and they remember.

So, while the Elysian's grand circular driveway, fountain, ballroom, guest rooms with gas fireplaces, and terraces all scream "heart-of-Paris-grandeur," the brand emanates from Pisor's real interest in creating a genuine experience. His philosophy is to make real connections. He defines luxury as something personal. Elysian is "all the things that make up me," he says.

STEP 1: FINDING *YOUR* STORIES

The David Pisor story should have you thinking about your own life story, which is actually a series of stories. Pisor's experiences have shaped a larger story, about who he is as a CEO and leader.

The questions that follow should elicit your stories. These are the events that are memorable to you. We will be exploring your brand values—the principles that have shaped you.

At this stage, just remember these events; don't worry about how important they were. Trust the process. The coaches in our firm at Bates Communications use this approach with great success. Don't judge the story. The story might be a funny or a tragic one, a story of a failure or a success. Don't worry how "big" or "small" the event was. Just start writing.

Get into a quiet place and answer the following 10 questions. Give yourself at least 30 minutes for the exercise. Read each question, close your eyes, and note whatever comes into your mind. When you write, don't record the entire story yet. Jot down a sentence or two. Later you'll recall and record more of the details.

PERSONAL STORY QUESTIONS

1. Tell me about a challenge or significant event in your childhood.

_____

_____

_____

_____

2. Tell me about someone in your early years who made an impact on you and why.

_____

_____

_____

_____

3. Recall a story from your early career—a significant event you share often with others.

_____

_____

_____

_____

4. Tell me about a time you got a promotion, or didn't, and how you felt.

_____

_____

_____

_____

5. Tell me about one of the most embarrassing, awkward, or difficult events in your career.

_____

_____

_____

_____

6. Share one of your greatest successes. What happened, and why do you remember it?

_____

_____

_____

_____

7. Share one of your greatest failures. What happened, and why do you remember it?

_____

_____

_____

_____

8. Tell me about a moment when you had to make a difficult decision, and what you did.

_____

_____

_____

_____

9. Tell me about a recent event that made you question yourself or a decision you had made.

_____

_____

_____

_____

10. Tell me about a person who is heavily influencing you right now.

_____

_____

_____

_____

Next Step

Now that you have identified a few potential "brand discovery" story ideas, it's time to examine what those stories mean to you. Often, events in early in life may not seem that important, until you examine them. Often as you recall these events, you discover they were essential to the formation of your character. In interviewing leaders, it became clear to me that many of the significant, brand-shaping events took place early in their lives. That's why it is important to go all the way back through your early years to examine what happened and why it was important to you.

George Colony, CEO, Forrester Research

George Colony grew up in small-town New Hampshire, second to last in a family of seven children. Several generations of his family owned the textile mill in town, going all the way back to the Civil War. They amassed a considerable amount of wealth; however, by the time his father's generation took over, the mill was struggling, and after some agonizing years, it went out of business in 1979. "It was a weird existence," he says. "We owned the mill; everyone in town worked in the mill and lived in houses owned by my family. But we had no money in the family." Colony felt most closely connected to the kids whose mothers and fathers worked in the factory. "We were all in this together."

Colony's lessons in business didn't just come out of the failure of the family business, though. He observed his uncle, David Putnam, who was not in the mill business. "He was fantastic with people, very fair," Colony recalls. His uncle walked the factory floor, as comfortable there as in a boardroom. "He took care of his workers, revolutionizing the business by moving hourly workers to salary with health-care benefits. He wasn't a mentor—he was an example."

After Harvard, Colony wanted to be an entrepreneur. He launched Forrester Research in 1983, and grew it into a global technology and market research company. Today the company trades on the Nasdaq, has been ranked among Forbes 200 Best Small Companies, and has twice been named to the *Boston Globe*'s list of Top Places to Work. Its worldwide offices include Australia, Canada, Dubai, France, Germany, India, Israel, The Netherlands, Switzerland, and the United Kingdom.

> "He took care of his workers, revolutionizing the business by moving hourly workers to salary with health–care benefits. He wasn't a mentor—he was an example."

Colony is never afraid to take a position on an issue. This trait sealed his reputation as a thought leader in technology and drove value into his company brand. He's made provocative predictions, such as the dot-com implosion and the rise of social computing. He's been invited to partici- pate in the World Economic forums in Davos, Switzerland. Speaking courageously became a brand value of Forrester. Colony models the trait. "If I'm not courageous," he asks, "why would a Forrester analyst want to be?" At the same time, the Forrester/Colony brand is down to earth. He treats the administrative assistant the same way he treats the COO. "The idea of special parking spots and privileges for the CEO—I've always hated those ideas," he says.

Forrester has an open, shared work group space. There's no CEO office with a door. Colony works in the pod workspaces, just like everybody else. He sees his company as a "dream machine." "If you have a dream and it aligns with Forrester's dream, you have a place here," Colony says.

STEP 2: TELL THE STORY

As you read Colony's story, the foundation of his brand becomes clear early in his life. These childhood events shaped who he has become. Now it's time for you to take the next step; to examine your stories in greater depth. Choose one story, and determine what that experience is telling you about your values.

Once you've chosen one of the stories, find a friend, and ask that person to listen to your story and ask you questions. I strongly recommend that you get a digital recorder so you have a record of the conversation. *Tell him or her the story.* If you don't have a coach or friend to help you, record the story, and play it back. I urge you not to sit at your computer and write; tell your story out loud. Why? Most people do not find it possible to capture all that is important in a story when they are writing. They edit as they go and leave out important details that only emerge while writing "out loud." I have worked with leaders for years and found that "writing out loud" is the secret to capturing those details that will lead you to the truth of the story. I've provided 20 questions in the inset box to prompt those insights. Ask yourself these questions, or have your partner ask them.

20 "STORY QUESTIONS"

1. What year was it?
2. Where were you?
3. Describe the surroundings.
4. Who was there?
5. Why were you there?
6. Can you explain that further?
7. Who said what to whom?
8. Why did you say that?
9. Why did he or she say that?
10. Why was that significant?
11. How did you feel?
12. How did you react?
13. What had you expected?
14. Why did it turn out that way?
15. What was the outcome?
16. What was the impact?
17. Why do you remember this?
18. Do you have any regrets?
19. What did you learn?
20. Why is this relevant?

If you do have a friend, coach, or trusted advisor helping you, ask that person to think of this as an interview, and give her permission to interrupt you as you go through the story. Tell the interviewer to stop and ask questions any time she hears something she doesn't understand. Don't allow her to jump to any conclusions until all the questions have been asked. You should also resist the temptation to jump to conclusions. Don't assume you know what the story is about before you have thoroughly examined the details through these questions.

Brand "Story" Writing Tips

Here are a few pieces of advice for writing your story:

- Regarding the scope—keep it narrow. A story is a *snapshot in time*. Don't tell the *history* of your career. You want to break it up into episodes or vignettes. The story about George Colony is really several stories. If I were interviewing him with these questions, I would choose just one event, such as a time when he observed his uncle at work, and I would explore it further. That's what you should do. Choose one moment, and go deep.
- As you speak, picture the scene in your mind's eye. Describe it. Take us there. Tell us who said what to whom. Imagine you're writing a scene in a movie or an act in a play.
- Focus on the critical moment, when things came together. Your lesson will emerge from there. It may be something small such as a comment someone made or an observation you had. The more specific you are about that moment, the easier it will be to draw a clear lesson from the experience.

Not every detail will make it into the story, but capture them all now and sort them out later. The best approach is to write down everything, and then go back when you are fresh and analyze what was most important. Working with a communications coach or a writer may help you accelerate this process as they are able to ask questions and reflect back an observation you may not have thought of before.

Next Step

Let's look at one more story about a leader who has built a great company and a strong personal brand. Again, read for inspiration that will remind you about the key moments of your own stories that translate into powerful leadership lessons.

Diane Hessan, Communispace

"I grew up on the wrong side of the tracks, so I always had a lemonade stand and sold the most Girl Scout cookies," says Diane Hessan, CEO and founder of Communispace, a successful marketing company with clients such as Coca-Cola, Home Depot, Hewlett-Packard, Mattel, Best Buy, FedEx, and Campbell's Soup that hire the firm to help them get closer to their customers.

Hessan's father made a modest living in a sewing machine repair business. As a child, she volunteered to work in her dad's store, waiting on customers and even coordinating a direct mail campaign for the store at age 13.

Hessan had a natural affinity for business. She felt comfortable leading at an early age. "I was captain of a sports team and didn't play the whole season. I wasn't a great athlete, but I liked doing the captain thing," she recalls.

Graduating from a high school just outside Philadelphia, with a class of 800, Hessan says only two students went to college out of state, and the most popular job after high school was UPS truck driver. Hessan had to be creative about her future, so she cobbled together financial aid and worked her way through Tufts University, graduating summa cum laude. Then, she attended a seminar on getting your MBA, and decided to write her application to Harvard Business School in *calligraphy*. "I knew it was going to be hard to stand out," she says. "I also told them I am almost out of money, so if you defer me, I can't come."

> "I was captain of a sports team. . . . I wasn't a great athlete, but I liked doing the captain thing," [Hessan] recalls.

She was accepted to Harvard at the age of 20.

It would be two decades before she started her own company. She didn't make CEO of the company she worked for, so she started dreaming about doing "her own thing." The "captain" needed a team to lead. She chose technology, though she didn't know a server from a piece of silverware, so she decided to create collaborative software to build communities of employees working virtually in their companies.

It was a struggle at first, but on a "lucky day" a client suggested to Hessan that she try a new approach: repurpose the software to help companies create "community" with their *customers*. It worked. But then, the Internet bubble burst. The company was down to enough cash for only a few months. Hessan brought her employees together and asked them for suggestions. They came back with over 50, including a voluntary, across-the-board salary reduction. People were so committed, they said they would be the last to turn out the lights. "It was moving to be part of an experience like that," she says.

The company survived until Thanksgiving, and then it turned the corner.

The Communispace brand is creative; it reminds you of the days when Hessan took out her calligraphy pen and applied to Harvard. It's also hard-driving, like Hessan. Hessan's true-grit brand is all over Communispace and the people who work there today.

STEP 3: ANALYZE THE STORY

Again, what you have just read is not one story but a compilation of several stories that have led Hessan to become the leader she is today. I wanted to weave them together so that you could see some larger lesson and themes.

Now we'll take part of her story and analyze it using the Bates Six-Part Story Structure (see Figure 3.1). This model is inspired by the great work of a number of influential speakers and storytellers I know. First and foremost, I am influenced by the work of Doug Stevenson, a member of the National Speakers Association. Although I have not taken Stevenson's storytelling course, his work on story structure has influenced my work and inspired this model. Over the years, in coaching leaders, I have developed it further

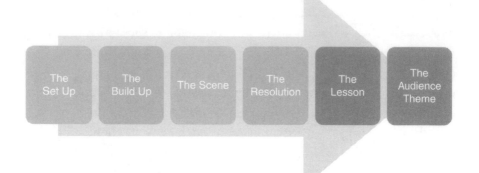

Figure 3.1 The Bates Six-Part Story Structure

to be effective for our clients. In addition, I want to acknowledge how other great storytellers have influenced my work, among them Patricia Fripp, Lou Heckler, and Marcia Reynolds. Each of them has been a coach and a mentor to me, with their own style and approach to storytelling. I am grateful for the lessons I've learned and hope that their work with me will help others.

The following is an example of how I might use these six elements to structure the Diane Hessan story.

The Setup

"I always had a lemonade stand," says Hessan. "Growing up, in grade school, I was the girl who always sold the most Girl Scout cookies. I grew up on the wrong side of the tracks. My dad had a sewing machine repair business. My grandfather owned a little newsstand. But it's funny, I had the business bug. Whenever I went to visit my grandfather, the first thing I did was run to the cash register, press the old-fashioned keys, and make it ring.

The Buildup

"When I graduated from high school, I wanted to go to college, but I didn't have the money. In my graduating class, the most popular job upon graduating was UPS driver; only 2 of 800 actually went to college out of state.

"But I really wanted to go. I had to get creative. So I cobbled together enough financial aid to go to Tufts University and worked my way through school in less than three years. I was a good student, graduating summa cum laude. But I was 20 years old, and I couldn't see the next step. Didn't know what to do with that degree.

The Scene

"A friend of mine came by one day and said, 'I'm going to a seminar on getting your MBA. Do you want to come?' 'I've never really thought about that,' I said. 'I'm not sure.' But I didn't have much to do that day, so I went along. As I sat in that seminar, suddenly a lightbulb went off. I wanted to go to business school. And I wanted to go to the best business school I knew of—Harvard University. The competition was, of course, ridiculous. I knew somehow I'd have to stand out. So I sat down and wrote the application, the entire thing, in calligraphy, and sent it off.

The Resolution

"I waited on pins and needles, until finally the envelope arrived. My heart was racing as I opened the letter. I had already told them that I was almost out of money, so if they had deferred me, I wouldn't be able to come. The first words I saw were, 'Diane, congratulations!' I didn't need to go further. At age 20 I had somehow managed to get myself into Harvard Business School.

The Lesson

"What I learned from that experience is how important it is to approach problems creatively. You can never allow circumstances to shape or define your goals. If you have limited resources, find a creative way to get what you want. I am grateful to have learned how to be creative and solve problems.

The Audience Theme (Her Employees)

"As I look around this organization, I'm proud of the fact that we have that same value here. We are creative in the way we face challenges. Many of you here today were on the team that decided to stay when we were almost broke; together we found a way to keep the lights on. We are a resourceful, creative, can-do organization. We never allow obstacles to get in the way of achieving our goals."

SIX-PART STORY STRUCTURE

The Setup
Who, what, when, where; take us to the scene with a few quick descriptions.

_____

_____

_____

The Buildup
Conflict, challenge, circumstance, obstacle, difficulty, or situation

_____

_____

_____

The Scene
Conversation, action, big moment, decision, choice; we should feel suspense.

_____

_____

_____

The Resolution
What happened; how did it turn out; and what was the result, outcome, or final decision?

_____

_____

_____

The Lesson
What you learned, saw, experienced, came to believe; this is a personal reflection; don't be the "hero"; instead, share a lesson.

_____

_____

_____

The Audience Theme

How does this lesson apply to this particular audience? Different audience, different theme, analogous to their circumstances, challenges, or situations

_____

_____

_____

WHY A LESSON *AND* AN AUDIENCE THEME?

In our boot camps and workshops, I'm often asked why it is important to find both a personal lesson and theme for the audience. Think of them this way:

- **The Lesson** is what *you* took away from the experience. It often begins with "What I learned . . ." or "What I discovered . . ." or "What I took away from that experience. . . ."
- **The Audience Theme** is how that lesson *applies* to a *particular* audience. The audience theme may change depending, upon who is out there listening. The question you are answering is, "How does this relate to me?" or "How is your experience connected to mine?" The answer to that question may be slightly or radically different, depending upon who is listening. The same story may require a different audience theme, depending upon who is in that audience.

As it relates to your brand, the lesson is the core piece. The audience theme is the way you will make that lesson relevant to others. In leadership, you need to understand the lesson you learned, which is part of your brand, and then communicate it, in a way that is meaningful to each audience. This last piece, the audience theme, is important to others. When you hit on the right audience theme, it is highly motivating and inspiring for others. This is where as a leader you connect your experience to theirs.

NOW, TRY IT

Go back and look at one of your stories. What was the lesson? Start the sentence with

"What I learned was . . ."

_____

_____

_____

_____

Now think of an audience or person who might hear that story—perhaps leaders or managers in your organization.

> In workshops, I've watched leaders who didn't believe they had a single story to tell, stand up and share something that leaves their audiences breathless.

You might want to start with a phrase like "What I see today in our company is how we too can . . ."

_____

_____

_____

_____

A SIGNATURE STORY ABOUT YOUR PERSONAL BRAND

If you've been successful with this exercise, what you have just written might well become a signature story of your personal leadership brand. Not only should it help you understand your own brand, you should be able to share those lessons and make them relevant to others. Perhaps you've told the story before, but never with a powerful lesson that brought clarity for you and meaning to the listener. Now you should understand why it is important and how you can use it to communicate your brand.

How many stories do you have? In a short time you have identified several. As you become a strong storyteller, you'll see how the events of your life, when examined, become opportunities to share lessons and the values that define your brand. The more you use this tool, the more you'll think about stories and what they mean to you and others. In workshops, I've watched leaders who didn't believe they had anything to say, stand up and tell stories that leave their audiences breathless. What's fascinating is that often they have told these stories to people they know and not realized they had greater meaning. The storytelling structure helps you not only organize your story, but also analyze it to find a lesson and a relevant point for your audience. This "aha!" moment is exciting and easy to replicate, once you apply the storytelling formula. I've seen it happen so many times in our workshops that I've come to expect it. The process really works.

CONNECTING THE STORY OF YOU TO THE STORY OF YOUR COMPANY

As you look at your story, you may begin to see a correlation between the values that are important to you and the values that have shaped your company and its culture. If you don't see a correlation, that's something to note; either there is a misalignment between your brand and the company brand, or you have work to do, communicating the lessons and values that you believe can create value in your organization.

One way to test the resonance between your own brand and your company brand is to look for the evidence that your brand values are living in the organization. Now that you have identified lessons and values important to you through your stories, how do see those reflected in the actions and behaviors of others? What have you noticed about the way they approach challenges or situations that is aligned with what you believe is important? What have you noticed about the way your team works together, overcomes obstacles, and meets objectives that is consistent with the values you believe in?

HOW TO SHARE "BRAND" STORIES

As you go down the path of building a brand, your stories will become a powerful communication tool, helping you to highlight lessons and values.

You will be able to explain who you are as a leader, and what defines you, through these stories. People enjoy hearing stories; they remember stories and therefore remember the lessons. If you have struggled, failed, made bad choices or mistakes, these can be the best stories of all. Sharing those stories about facing obstacles creates a strong bond when you make it relevant to what people are facing today.

I am constantly astounded at the stories I hear in our workshops and our executive coaching programs. From survival at sea, to being born in an orphanage, to trekking to the highest mountain peaks, I've watched "ordinary leaders" amaze their audiences with incredible tales. These are character-revealing stories that explain so much about who they are and have relevance for their audiences. We *all* have interesting stories to tell. That's life! It's darn interesting! And you don't have to have been in prison, or fought a war, or survived a life-threatening event to have great stories that are meaningful to others.

When you have found these stories, share them with others. They can be the inspiration for shaping the character and values of your team. In your presentations, interviews, and writing, seek to create an emotional connection through stories. Keep coming back to this process and building your anthology of signature leadership stories—the stories of you. If you find it challenging at first, work with a partner, coach, or speechwriter to shorten the process and produce great results.

Now that you've completed this very important step, it's time to look at how your brand can become known to others. Let's move on to examine how people know you, the leader.

CHAPTER SUMMARY

- The best way to understand your brand is to look at stories from your life.
- As you analyze these stories, you'll find lessons that have defined you.
- Use questions to go deep into those stories and find the point.
- Don't judge your stories or try to guess what they are telling you.
- Get someone to interview you, or ask yourself questions to help you get to the lesson.
- Use the techniques in this chapter to find audience themes that convey your brand values.
- Collect and tell signatures stories that represent your brand.

Brand Recognition—What Do People Say about You?

Everything a CEO says and does is no longer personal.
It is attributed to the company.

—SHELLY LAZARUS, CEO, OGILVY & MATHER

O NCE YOU HAVE RECORDED AND ANALYZED your stories, and discovered the values that emerge, you can begin to communicate your brand. A clear understanding of these values makes it simple to share with others. Consider the leaders you have met in this book. They know what they are all about; they can, therefore, communicate their brand values. This makes a profound impact on the organizations they lead. Imagine the impact you can have when you are just as clear about the values that define your brand.

What you communicate about your brand values determines what people come to know, expect, and believe about you. If I asked people who know you to describe you—from employees, to partners, colleagues, customers, shareholders, analysts, the media, professional associates, and influential people what would they say? Are you communicating what you intend to communicate about your brand?

As you get clarity, you can communicate clearly, and a picture emerges of you. People get to know you, and appreciate what you stand for.

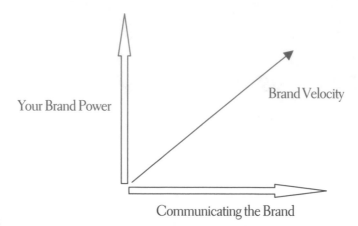

Figure 4.1 Brand Velocity

That clarity about you creates brand *velocity* (see Figure 4.1). Velocity is the rate of speed at which your brand gains traction and makes an impact. The greater the clarity about your brand, and the better you communicate, the faster your brand builds, the more rapidly you can make an impact on the organization.

Early in their careers, many leaders don't realize that they have a brand, and they don't stop to think about the power that brand has in influencing others and driving a business result. They don't understand how potent their brand can be, in building a great organization. Nevertheless, over time, these leaders discover that the values they hold dear are alive and well in their organizations. They come to appreciate how these brand values are defining their companies and driving their businesses forward.

JOE GUSTAFSON, CEO, BRAINSHARK

Joe Gustafson is one of those guys that never had an interest in building a personal brand. He wanted to build a business. As the founder of Brainshark, Gustafson eats, breathes, and lives his company. He loves business. It's never been about him. Brainshark creates multimedia presentations from PowerPoint slides, documents, and Web pages. Gustafson is a self-effacing leader who always gives credit to his team for the company's success. Yet there's no question that Gustafson's brand lives in the organization and has accelerated his success.

How the Brand Developed

Gustafson became an entrepreneur at age 29 when he founded an earlier company, Relational Courseware Inc. (RCI); he says that when he started he had no idea what he was doing. "You learn as you go. We started out of my condo in the Back Bay of Boston. My girlfriend—who's now my wife—was a very good salesperson, so she supported us while I started the business."

Gustafson had a strong proclivity to keep an eye on his cash (unlike many startup technology entrepreneurs). "For a while you can fund [your company] on a credit card and dig into your own pocket," he says. "As you hire more people, you can't do that."

Gustafson's cash flow management required persistence and creativity. For example, when he won a big client, Oracle, he was thrilled, but he soon realized they had "mastered the process of stretching out their accounts payable." Gustafson's got to know the people who could get the check in his hands, taking them out to dinner, to bowl, or to play miniature golf. "They would fill me in on whose desk [my check] was sitting on," he says. "Anything over $50,000 had to be signed by Larry Ellison, and they would make sure it got done and into a Federal Express envelope on its way."

Lesson Learned

What did he learn from that? "The basic approach I took was to be creative in solving the problem," says Gustafson. "If you run out of cash, your business is gone. Cash is everything."

> "The basic approach I took was to be creative in solving the problem." says Gustafson.

Though the company was venture backed, Gustafson's bootstrap mentality saved it from going under. He recalls that "it was February,

Presidents' Day weekend, and we were burning $800,000 a month. My wife and I went skiing with five other couples." One of his friend's eyes got as wide as saucers when he explained their burn rate. "I thought it was a badge of honor; he thought it was nuts. So I came back and talked to my directors."

They laid off 30 people, then a lot more, and then, the dot-com bubble burst. "I'm convinced that what we did saved the company," he says. From that day on, Gustafson drove home the value of prudent management: "I would go to every meeting and talk about managing like a bootstrap company. That infused the culture with good business practices."

What People "Buzz" about at Brainshark

Today the employees of Brainshark "know" these values. Gustafson is open with employees about the company's finances, in good times and bad. "We've had meetings and I told them how much money we had, what we were going to do, where we were going, how we were going to get there," he recalls. This openness reinforces the company values. The more he has talked about this, the more the value has been reinforced, the greater velocity of his brand. Today it is an essential aspect of the Brainshark culture.

Another brand value that starts with Gustafson's brand value is creativity. Largely because Gustafson is a creative guy, Brainshark has become a creative culture. You see it in the company's philanthropic efforts. Employees are allowed to design their own charitable giving program through the company's Shark Angels program. They take a paid day off to work, for a charity of their choice. The program was an employee's idea. Company employees go off with a $100 check from Brainshark, and they come back and make a short presentation about the experience using Brainshark's presentation software.

Encouraging employees to come up with their own creative ideas is a significant advantage in a company as innovative as Brainshark. The message is: we want and need your ideas. This trait now defines Brainshark's culture.

Gustafson showed me a presentation that an employee had just forwarded to him. The subject line read: "My Volunteer Day." "I spent yesterday at *Project Just Because*," writes the employee, "and they were thrilled to have an extra pair of hands and very grateful for the $100 donation. If you have a minute, you can hear more about the experience." That's what I mean by buzz. The employees now "own" that value—creativity—and want to share it with their boss and others. This generates brand velocity.

ASSESSING BRAND VELOCITY

When you see the values living in a company, you can be sure the leader's brand has velocity. The core values are taking hold and creating a good business outcome. The leader's values are becoming part of the DNA of the organization, driving value. The better you communicate your values, the greater brand velocity you build, and the more powerful and positive the impact on the organization.

How do you know whether you have brand velocity? In the sidebar, you'll find an exercise that will help you analyze yours. Think about an important event in your company recently. It may have been a big win, a challenge, or a response to a crisis. Analyze the story and discover what it is telling you. What is the value or principle that allowed people to overcome the obstacle or be successful? And how does that connect back to the values you have identified as important to you?

BRAND VELOCITY ASSESSMENT

Write down the values that emerged in your leadership stories in Chapter 3.

_____

_____

_____

_____

_____

_____

_____

Now, think about an important event in your company in the last three months. Perhaps it was a big win, a great response to a crisis, a challenge, or an obstacle. Do you see a connection to one of the above values?

Yes

No

If yes, tell the story and connect it to the value.

_____

_____

_____

_____

_____

_____

_____

_____

WHAT IF YOU DON'T SEE IT?

If you haven't yet seen a connection between people's actions and these brand values, you may want to examine a few more similar situations to see if you can find a theme. If you aren't able to identify the values that are driving your success, get together with a small group of leaders on your team and go through this exercise. This is an excellent team-building opportunity, and you may want to bring in a facilitator or coach.

If you don't see the values that you want to see coming through, it's time to think about how to bring them into the culture. In what ways can you communicate these values or behaviors so that they become part of your company's DNA? Remember, good management practices weren't part of Joe Gustafson's culture until he started talking about it and reinforcing the message on a weekly basis.

Write down a value here that, if you were to be successful in communicating it, would drive value into your company:

_____

_____

_____

_____

MAKING IT HAPPEN

It is important to document and communicate the values, as part of the success formula for your organization. By identifying the values, and then developing a communications plan, you will be successful in making them real, and eventually, you will see them at work every day. It isn't enough to communicate with plaques on the wall, you have to talk about the values, and live the values. This is how people begin to believe them, remember them, and act on them.

How do you know your values are living in the enterprise? You are able to point to specific examples where you see them at work in your company. You are able to trace back what is happening to the way people are acting on principles and beliefs. You also begin to attract and retain people who share and act on the same values. You are also able to identify and say good-bye to people who are not a fit, because they don't act on the values. You also begin to attract the kinds of clients and customers you want because they want to do business with a company like yours. The same is true of investors, shareholders, and partners.

THE ROAD DEVELOPING YOUR BRAND—BARBARA LYNCH

A brand value emerges over a period of time; sometimes it takes years to understand it and communicate it effectively. Barbara Lynch grew up in the Mary Ellen McCormack housing project in South Boston, the sixth of seven kids. Her father died a month before she was born. Lynch was a "ringleader" with her gang of friends (whom she is still friendly with today). "Even when I was seven or eight, people believed in me and would do whatever I said," says Lynch. "It's just who I am."

School was a disaster; in the era of forced bussing in Boston, Lynch ended up at Madison Park High School, which she describes as a racial war zone. She became a troublemaker, with no discipline. "In my math class, I was a bookie," she says. "My teachers would give me money to bet on the dogs, but I wouldn't call in the bet, I would spend the money on clothes. It wasn't like we had after-school programs."

The only class Lynch attended was home economics, where a teacher took interest in her; cooking was the reason she stayed in school.

To make money, she got a job at a club where her mother worked. She was impressed by the dinner parties for club members. When her mother cooked at home, Barbara Lynch could tell the meat was done by the smell.

Out of high school, Lynch got a warehouse job on the docks. Her best friend finally came to meet her and said, "You've got to get outta here." Lynch quit and took a trip on a credit card, then took a cooking job on Martha's Vineyard where, she says, "I was working 80 hours opening cans and pouring them."

When a chance to cook on a dinner cruise boat came along, Lynch was asked if she could make lobster and filet mignon; she lied and said yes. "I went to the library and bought books on how to butcher meat," she says. The boat gig was successful, and Lynch "fell in love with the creativity of cooking."

Then came a break. Lynch was hired by celebrity chef Todd English, and became a student of food, sassy and independent, but pushing herself to learn. "I would go home every night and read *Foods of Italy* by Waverly Root," relates Lynch. She again borrowed a friend's credit card, went to Italy, and tasted real Bolognese sauce and Italian prosciutto. She cooked with an Italian woman and vowed she would master the art. After winning a major award, celebrated chef Gordon Hamersley called to advise her, "Don't waste this opportunity." She opened her own place, No. 9 Park, in Boston.

Communicating the Brand to Your Team

Lynch recalls that "I hired some of the best servers in the city, but they didn't like the way I wanted it done. For example, I wanted to change the silver at each course [rather than creating an intimidating set of utensils across the table] but it was a lot of work for them."

Lynch wanted great food but not an intimidating atmosphere for customers.

It was a moment of truth—one that defined her leadership and set the course for her success. She closed the restaurant on Friday, called a mandatory meeting of the staff, and made it clear that they should return only if they could do it the No. 9 Park way. I will give you the weekend," she told them, "but you are not going to run my restaurant. If you don't like it, don't come back on Monday." Some people didn't come back; those who did were now as committed as she was. No. 9 Park became a huge success—people were buzzing. Her brand started gaining velocity, which is so essential in the world of celebrity chefs.

Today, Lynch has eight other restaurant properties, or "concepts," from Menton, a glamorous fine-dining destination named after a French village on the Italian border, to the Butcher Shop, a wine bar and restaurant with a full-service European style "boucherie," to B&G Oysters, a neighborhood oyster bar with amazingly fresh seafood. Each is known for its unique atmosphere, great service, and, of course, fabulous food.

> *"Barbara Lynch would never bake a tough cookie, but she is one, for sure. Lynch, 44, balled on high school and was a runner for local bookies before nestling under the wing of celebrity chef Todd English. A James Beard Award–winner, she has built Barbara Lynch Gruppo (formerly No. 9 Group) into a more than $10 million amalgam of six high-concept restaurants and food businesses. She expects revenue to double with three new ventures: a '50s-style cocktail bar, a reimagined lunch counter, and the hautest haute cuisine restaurant to touch down in Boston. 'Not bad for a kid from the projects,' says Lynch."*
>
> —Inc. *magazine, 2008*

Lynch's brand is evident in every restaurant: the vision, the creativity, the quality, and the love for Italian and French food. She now earns rave comments like the one in the sidebar. What a story!

A Signature Brand Story

Yes, Barbara Lynch's amazing personal story is a signature of her brand. As you have discovered, you also have signature stories. Your story is your story, your brand is your brand, and you simply need to be aware of it and communicate it in order to create brand velocity.

At first, Lynch didn't have brand velocity. She was reluctant to be a brand. What mattered to her were the restaurants, the business, and the people. However, as she matured as a leader, she realized it was just good business to amplify the brand. So she started to "come out of the kitchen" and do media interviews.

So, for Lynch, the secret to beginning to build brand velocity was embracing her brand and being willing to tell her story, the real story, in a compelling way. And this story provides the authenticity for her brand.

People are curious about who you are and where you came from! Don't be shy about sharing it and drawing the lessons from it that are relevant to others. As people learn about you and what is different about your leadership it creates an excitement, or buzz, that accelerates brand awareness and velocity.

BELIEVE IN YOURSELF—TORY BURCH

Whatever you do, you must believe in your brand. No one but you can get behind your own brand and communicate it the way you will, as people may not always embrace your brand from the start. When famed fashion designer Tory Burch opened her first boutique store, many people in her own Manhattan socialite circles dismissed it as a vanity project. Burch was a socialite, on the short list of "who's who" people you'd want at a big event. She had studied art history at the University of Pennsylvania and spent the 1990s doing marketing and public relations for Ralph Lauren and Vera Wang by day, making the party scene by night.

But Burch believed in her brand—she knew it had value. When she opened in Manhattan's Nolita district with a $2 million investment courtesy of her then-husband (who remains an investor today), the fashion magazines and gossip rags raved. Burch was one of *them*. Friends from the New York social scene mobbed the store. It wasn't long before Oprah Winfrey discovered Tory Burch, and the rest was history. By 2010 her company was projecting $300 million in sales and was planning to open 100 stores worldwide.

"There were a lot of eyebrows raised when I said I wanted to start this company," she told *Bloomberg* in an interview, "and many people thought it would be a vanity project." Tory Burch ignored all that and decided to be who she was. She knew her style, and she ignored the critics who were probably just envious. She wore her own fashions and modeled the retro-cool, modern bohemian fashions that women now love. Brand velocity started with a belief in herself.

So, there you have stories about two different women, one who grew up with privilege, one who had to overcome huge obstacles, both with brand velocity. They are who they are; they embrace that and communicate it to others in their own ways. What about you? What's the story you need to share? How could that create brand velocity for you?

WHERE ARE YOU NOW?

It's a good idea to assess awareness of your brand as you set out to increase your brand velocity. One way to do that is to review what people say about you. That includes what is reported in the media, through articles, bylines, and interviews. If you are just beginning to build a public brand, and you haven't had much publicity, that's okay. This is a good time to start thinking about how you want to communicate your brand in the media, and to the public.

If you are not seeking to build a public profile, there are other places to find clues to how your leadership brand is perceived internally. For example, you can look at performance reviews and 360 interview reports. You can also ask colleauges or friends to complete the Trusted Advisor Survey that I provided for readers in my first book, *Speak Like a CEO*.

Once you have ascertained how the public or key people internally, currently perceive your brand, the next step is to write down what you would *like* people to say about you—words that are closely aligned with the way you now think about your brand. Use one of the two forms in the following sidebars to write it out the way you'd like to see it. The first is a 100-word "story" like the one that *Inc.* magazine wrote about Barbara Lynch. The second is a simple Self-Performance Review form that could be used in a performance review.

INC. MAGAZINE

Date:

Title:

(100 words)

_____
_____
_____
_____
_____
_____
_____
_____
_____
_____
_____
_____
_____
_____
_____
_____
_____

SELF-PERFORMANCE REVIEW

What I would like people to say about me:

Values I live by:

_____
_____
_____

Three words I would like people to use to describe me:

How people know this about me:

THINKING ABOUT YOUR CORE BRAND—KATHERIN NUKK-FREEMAN

When Katherin Nukk-Freeman and her friend decided to open a law practice, they had already been lawyers in big firms. They knew they wanted to do law differently. Rather than grinding down new associates with 80- to 100-hour workweeks, they started planning two years in advance to create a company where people could thrive.

The tagline they wrote before they even opened the doors to Nukk-Freeman & Cerra, P.C., was "Teaming with Employers to Build a Better Workplace." What that meant to them wasn't just keeping their employees happy but also educating their clients about how to stay out of trouble. Says Nukk-Freeman: "We really established the firm with the mindset that we want to give proper advice on how to manage employees, including how to pay people, grant them leaves, accommodate disabilities, and prevent harassment."

By thinking this through in advance, Nukk-Freeman was able to start fresh, with an approach that would win client loyalty. She and her friend would build long-term relationships with grateful clients who didn't have to go broke defending themselves in court. And they would create a pleasant, productive, supportive environment for attorneys and staff.

How the Company Communicates to Create Buzz

Nukk-Freeman shares the message you see in the sidebar about how she does business with every client. The firm's philosophy is in her bio, on its website, and in its newsletter, and it is part of the conversations Nukk-Freeman's attorneys have with their clients. The company frequently sends e-mail to inform clients about changes in legislation to keep them from making mistakes with employees. All of those things constantly reinforces the message and creates brand velocity.

KATHERIN NUKK-FREEMAN

Katherin Nukk-Freeman devotes a majority of her practice to the counseling of clients on diverse employment issues, including those pertaining to family and medical leaves, wage and hour requirements, compliance with the Consolidated Omnibus Budget Reconciliation Act (COBRA), discrimination laws, hiring and termination decisions, drug testing, and state and federal disability laws. Nukk-Freeman also trains employees of all levels including nonsupervisory employees, supervisory employees, human resources professionals, and upper management with respect to all of the aforementioned areas.

She also works with clients to develop and draft employment procedures, contracts, and handbooks that fit their business needs. Nukk-Freeman utilizes her years of employment litigation experience to help her clients avoid litigation through effective and sound proactive business practices. Nukk-Freeman also has extensive experience representing management clients exclusively in disputes before administrative agencies [including state and federal Equal Employment Opportunity (EEO) agencies and the Department of Labor].

The Brand Attracts Top Talent

As the word became known about the firm, it was able to attract top talent. A family-friendly environment offered flexible work arrangements, another way to communicate the brand. Nukk-Freeman and her partner encouraged a "team approach" to client work, which provided additional flexibility and again reinforced the brand. "We've always said we strive to create an environment where people can be exceptional attorneys and exceptional people," she says.

How the Brand Buzz Drives Value

There are many ways that Nukk-Freeman and Cerra have watched their brand creating buzz and driving value into their business. Among them:

- As the firm focused on educating clients, fewer of them went to court, generating loyalty; even when clients were sued, they tended to be on solid ground, so defending them was easier, and the cases went their way, meaning that the attorneys were regarded as very successful.
- Success, of course, meant that clients voiced appreciation to their attorneys and staff for taking care of them and helping them do the right thing. The attorneys felt successful financially, but they also felt good about the way they helped their clients.
- This situation created longer-term relationships, as clients stayed with the firm. This meant Nukk-Freeman & Cerra, P.C, wasn't constantly on the hunt for business—it didn't see the churn.
- This stability further burnished the company's brand identity, and made its attorneys feel good about the practice of law. "We'd like to think we give lawyers a better reputation," says Nukk-Freeman.
- Both Nukk-Freeman, married with kids, and her partner married with kids, were able to meet their own family commitments, as were their employees.
- They attracted attorneys who would have been on a partner track at big-name firms. "At a large law firm it's a choice," says Nukk-Freeman. "You can be a good attorney or a good spouse/friend,

or you can be a good parent and be a mediocre attorney in their eyes at those firms. We wanted to attract A-plus players who could be exceptional in both areas."

Leveraging Your Brand Buzz to Keep Talent

Your personal brand is a huge factor in retaining top talent. As the saying goes, people join companies but they leave bosses. When people know what you stand for, and when they see it living in the culture, it creates positive buzz. What is the value of one great employee to your organization? Now multiply that by 10, or 100, or 1,000. If your brand velocity only lives inside the organization, it's worth a fortune to the company.

As most good employers know, compensation and benefits are the baseline for attracting and keeping talent. Winners want to work for winners, in companies where the brand values resonate. They can work anywhere. This is why your brand and culture have such tremendous value. You know your brand is buzzing when potential employees come in the door talking about you. You see it in their eyes. They are excited. "People are happy at our firm, and it really is a positive work culture," says Nukk-Freeman. Other firms "are notorious for having revolving doors," she adds. "We've avoided that, and gone from 2 to 18 attorneys, and we have zero attrition, or a 100 percent retention rate."

CREATING BUZZ BY LIVING THE VALUES—LISA MATTHEWS, FINANCIAL ADVISOR, WINSLOW, EVANS & CROCKER

Lisa Matthews has been a successful investment manager for 20 years. Her current firm, Winslow, Evans & Crocker is a full-service financial advisory firm with $3 billion in assets under management. She has a loyal following of individuals, families, businesses, and charitable foundations, who think of her services the way wealthy people think of a "family office," where they can receive helpful personal and financial advice.

Lisa describes her own brand as one of integrity. Her belief in living with integrity goes back to childhood. "When I was in second grade I was playing dodgeball," she recalls. "That was my favorite gym activity in elementary school. The kids on the other side weren't going out when they got hit by the ball. So I stopped playing the game and went to the other end of the gym to shoot hoops."

Her refusal to stay in the game earned a punitive trip to the principal's office, where she calmly tried to explain that she didn't want to play with kids who cheat. The principal called her parents; her mother showed up and asked the principal why they were there. Upon learning her daughter was being punished, Matthews' mother replied, "I believe you have the wrong child in your office."

How the Value Generates Brand Velocity

How is Matthews' brand communicated? She has a powerful network of friends, colleagues, and acquaintances who know her this way. Though she moved to Boston midcareer and didn't know anyone, she is today one of the best-known business people in the city. Matthews joined boards, volunteered on committees, and took on leadership positions, including leading two Women President Organization chapters. Her brand is well understood because she lives it. "Your brand is built not just in business, but in consistently living the brand in all parts of your life," says Matthews.

You cannot separate business life from the rest of your life when it comes to building a brand. You have to act consistently with your values in mind in every organization or group to which you belong. Whether you're a member of a condominium association, nonprofit board, school committee, church or synagogue, professional association, neighborhood group, it all has to be consistent. "My brand is who I am, no matter where I am, no matter what I'm doing, whoever I'm with, whoever is working for me, in my business," Matthews explains. "I'm the same in my business, in my community, on my boards, and with my family. It's very important."

> "I have a low threshold of tolerance for people who don't live by integrity. It's been my goal to have integrity since I started my business 21 years ago."

Matthews is choosy about the organizations she serves. When she gets involved and discovers integrity isn't a value, she finds a way to gracefully bow out. "It has to be aligned," she says. "I left a board because of this lack of alignment. I didn't feel the board was doing what it said it was going to do, according to its mission and values." In her business, investment advising, trust is too rare; her standards of integrity can't be high enough.

Matthews also shares her brand in her value statement, which she hands to every client and prospect. "Any time I take on a role or hire someone or work with a client, I have this discussion with them," she says. "We talk about my values and their values, and expectations and goals. There are times when I've walked away from strategic alliances, running other businesses, partnerships, or clients, and have fired clients because of a breach in the values or my brand."

Assess the "Fit" with Your Brand

If, like Lisa Matthews, you've been involved on boards and in organizations, you know that some have been a fit while others have not. You may have left those organizations because they were not aligned with your interests or your values. In fact, you may also have left a job for the same reason.

Be sure that all your associations sync up with your brand. If they aren't in sync, it creates disharmony, you are unhappy, you don't enjoy it, and it doesn't serve your brand well. The exercise in the sidebar will help you get clarity going forward about how to align yourself with organizations that are a fit.

ASSESS THE "FIT" WITH YOUR BRAND

Name of company, association, or nonprofit group:

_____

_____

What "values" or "characteristics" of this group initially attracted you?

_____

_____

Did your experience with the group affirm your initial impression and make you happy?

Yes

No

If yes, what was it about the group that aligned with your interests and values?

_____

_____

If no, what was happening that was out of alignment with your interests and values?

_____

_____

What did you learn from this experience that can help you choose organizations that are perfectly in sync with your leadership brand?

_____

_____

FINAL THOUGHTS ON WHAT PEOPLE SAY

Building a strong leader brand doesn't imply that everyone should like you or approve of you. Some people don't really know you, some people don't understand you, agree with you, or even care about you, and that's okay. Being a good leader doesn't require you to be a perfect person. Be true to your core values, live those values, and don't worry about naysayers. Leadership isn't a popularity contest. You don't have to be liked by *everyone*. Live by your brand values and stay with your own True North.

In coming chapters, we'll look at some detailed examples of how to put together a brand communication plan through traditional and new media. In the meantime, remember that, above all, to build a powerful brand, you have to be true to yourself. Never compromise.

Next, let's look at how you can leverage your brand once you have built it.

CHAPTER SUMMARY

- Your brand has velocity when you know your values and communicate well.
- Brand velocity speeds up progress on your important goals.
- Communicating your brand attracts people and opportunity.
- The story of you is interesting, and it will attract good press.
- You can't please everyone—most great leaders are controversial.
- Always be true to yourself and to the core of your brand.

Leveraging Your Brand
to Drive Spectacular Results

My greatest strength is really common sense. I'm a standard brand like Campbell's Tomato Soup or Baker's Chocolate.

—KATHARINE HEPBURN

EVERY DAY, YOU HAVE THE OPPORTUNITY to leverage your brand to drive value into your company. Actress Katharine Hepburn described her brand as common sense; you could see that brand in the iconic roles she played. She understood her own brand and leveraged it to build a legendary acting career. Whatever your brand, when you understand it and unleash it in the right setting, the impact is powerful and real. As you've learned from the stories of leaders in these chapters, a common thread is that they know who they are and how to communicate it to others. They understand their own brands, share those brand values, and shape the DNA of their organizations.

When the right leader is matched up with the right organization at the right time, the results are spectacular. It can be difficult for organizations and their directors to decide what type of leader is needed. Many times organizations go looking for a set of qualifications, only to reject candidates who fit those qualifications, and instead choose the leader who "feels" right at the time. The intuition about this choice is driven by a desire to hire for qualities that are difficult to find on a résumé, including the character, traits, and values that define that leader.

So the organization isn't looking only for a skill set but also for a set of traits and values that are a match for the current situation. Such was the case in January 2011, when Google announced that it would reshuffle the deck among the triumvirate who had always been its executive team. By then, Google had become the largest most powerful search engine in the world. CEO Eric Schmidt had been in charge for 10 years. He would step down to become executive chairman, and Larry Page would ascend again to CEO of the company he cofounded in 1998 with Sergey Brin.

Why was Larry Page tapped again to lead? Some analysts questioned whether he was ready to be in charge of such a large, complex, and important technology enterprise. Let's look at his story for the clues as to why the decision was made. The son of two computer scientists who taught at Michigan State University, he called his father a pioneer in artificial intelligence. When he was growing up, there were lots of *Popular Science* magazines lying around. He once built a printer from Legos. Page went off to Stanford University to pursue a Ph.D. in computer science, where he met and became friends with the eventual cofounder of Google, Sergey Brin.

Page has often given his supervisor at Stanford, Terry Winograd, credit for supporting him when he suggested his college project be to explore the mathematical properties of the World Wide Web. Who would attempt such a thing in college? It was a ridiculously complex idea for a student, but Winograd said yes to Page. Brin and Page eventually found a way to count and backlink Web pages, and then they came up with a PageRank algorithm that would be used to create a search engine superior to any other.

In a commencement speech at the undergrad alma mater University of Michigan, in May 2009, Page shared a few personal stories. He told the graduates and parents in attendance that success isn't just about following dreams. It's also finding a path to make those dreams real. He told a story about a summer camp program called LeaderShape, where he learned to "have a healthy disregard for the impossible."

As we all know there are many ge niuses who don't go off and build some of the world's largest most influential companies. The differentiating value for Page wasn't just his brain; it was his desire to achieve big, audacious goals. As the two cofounders built the company, the idea of big, audacious goals became inculcated in the culture. Google would attract other "geeks" who would be excited about doing something ridiculously, audaciously big. His brand—their brand—became the essence of the Google brand, and the basis of spectacular results.

"I think it is often easier to make progress on mega-ambitious dreams. I know that sounds completely nuts. But, since no one else is crazy enough to do it, you have little competition. There are so few people this crazy that I feel like I know them all by first name. They all travel as if they are pack dogs and stick to each other like glue. The best people want to work the big challenges. That is what happened with Google. Our mission is to organize the world's information and make it universally accessible and useful. How can that not get you excited? But we almost didn't start Google because my cofounder Sergey and I were too worried about dropping out of our Ph.D. program."
—Larry Page, Google cofounder, in a 2009
commencement speech to University of Michigan

WHY LEADERS ARE CHOSEN

Eric Schmidt put Google on a strong financial footing, but when it was announced that he would reclaim the CEO title, the sentiment was that the company had lost its technology edge. Competitors like Facebook threatened to siphon off users and advertising dollars. Having a strong balance sheet wasn't enough. The triumvirate appeared to want to move toward Page's brand of big thinking. Page's first months back in the CEO role in 2011 were marred by the perception that he blew the first quarter earnings call, dropping in to make a few scripted remarks, when most CEOs take charge and fully participate in these calls. It would remain to be seen whether Page would still be regarded as the right leader for what analysts have called the largest and most important technology company in the world.

The story never-the-less illustrates how at different times in the life of a company, different leaders rise, and one of the driving forces is whether their brand is in sync with what the company needs. There are plenty of skilled business leaders who might have the experience and background to run a company; however, the third determining factor is the leader's brand. What are the values and principles that have defined that leader, and how does it fit with where the company needs to go? When boards of directors and management teams seek the right leader, they must look at the values the individual embodies. They must seek the right leader with the right set of skills and values—a *brand*—who will take the organization in the right direction.

The next story illustrates how selecting the right leader with a brand that represents where the organization wants to go can turn things around and drive tremendous value into the enterprise.

ELLEN ZANE, TUFTS MEDICAL CENTER

When members of the board of Tufts Medical Center authorized a marketing study, they shouldn't have been surprised that the CEO they hired had a stronger brand than the institution she was now leading. Tufts Medical Center was faltering. Broke and struggling for an identity in the crowded world of Boston's elite teaching hospitals, Tufts New England Medical Center as it was known at that time needed a leader with talent and skill and her own formidable brand.

Zane would need every ounce of energy and creativity to turn it around. She would have to attract talent to the leadership team. One thing she had going for her was a great reputation with doctors.

Before we look at why her brand was the right one for the time, it may help to explain how the world of elite hospital care works. Physicians send patients with complex medical needs to hospitals affiliated with major centers, such as Harvard University. In Boston, a city replete with world-class health care, the competition for patients and doctor groups is fierce. The hospital needed a strong value proposition to sway community doctors to want to be affiliated with them.

Zane's reputation with doctors was burnished during 10 years with Partners Community Health, Inc. (PCHI), where she was known for building one of the largest physician networks in America. It had more than 1,000 internists, pediatricians, and family practice physicians and more than 3,500 specialists who provided care to more than 1.5 million patients.

Leveraging Relationships

Ellen Zane built and leveraged relationships by hitting the road and spending a lot of time with doctors. "I used to say I could be talking to a physician group in Haverhill in the morning and in Hyannis at night," she says. "We were in our cars, pounding the pavement. The strategy wasn't sexy. It was brick by brick, one doctor's office at a time."

Zane understood that doctors were afraid of being enveloped and subordinated by big academic institutions. She once went against her own company, PCHI, to woo one of the largest groups of doctors, Charles River Medical Associates. When PCHI suggested the doctors be forced to switch their allegiance on routine patient admissions, Zane recalls that "I said no."

So Zane's brand—trust and integrity—was built relationship by relationship, by being respectful of local community physicians. "My belief is that hospitals are bricks and mortar," says Zane. "I run a hospital with the philosophy that the doctors should be the navigator of care."

Leveraging the Brand in a New Organization

But would she be able to leverage this brand in a new hospital setting? Yes, in fact, her brand name would bring "oomph" to the flagging Tufts brand. Soon, the nearly bankrupt institution became the fastest-growing hospital in New England. In an otherwise flat market, between 2008 and 2010 Tufts Medical Center grew 21 percent under Zane, and the institution affiliated with Tufts Medical Center, The Floating Hospital of Boston also grew 28 percent.

What Zane brought to Tufts was a trusted brand with key constituencies who would help her turn things around.

One reason Zane was able to leverage her brand was because of another quality she values in herself—scrappiness. "My COO likes to talk about how if you come to be an executive here, you come to roll up your sleeves and wash the floor," says Zane. One of two girls born to a father who wanted sons, Zane says that "it was incredibly important to [my father] that my sister and I be independent and educated, so that no matter what life presented, we would be prepared." Her sister, Barbara, quit a company when she was passed over as CEO, started a competitive company, and sold it for $50 million. Yes, scrappiness was in their blood.

> The scrappy quality Zane brought began to permeate Tufts Medical Center. It was something she learned growing up in Waltham, Massachusetts, a blue-collar suburb of Boston.

Zane was able to leverage her scrappy, trusted brand because it was real. She has a confident, no-nonsense personal style that is utterly authentic. Leaders who leverage their brands have a great deal of confidence about how to wield that influence to drive value, as Zane has. Not only did Tufts regain its financial footing, Zane's brand gave the institution a new, more powerful identity.

You might think of the power of this leverage like what's illustrated in Figure 5.1. When business and competitive forces put downward pressure on

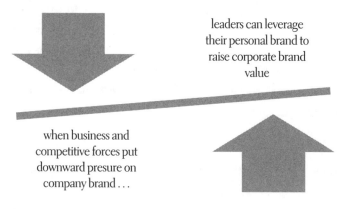

leaders can leverage their personal brand to raise corporate brand value

when business and competitive forces put downward presure on company brand . . .

Figure 5.1 How Leaders Can Leverage a Strong Brand

a company brand (the left side of the equation), a leader can leverage his or her own personal brand to raise the corporate brand value (the right side). It's amazing what the right CEO can do to drive value into a company by leveraging the power of his or her own brands. The next story is another example.

GAIL GOODMAN, CEO, CONSTANT CONTACT

Another leader who has successfully leveraged her personal brand for the benefit of the company is Gail Goodman, CEO of Constant Contact. If you're a small business leader, chances are you're familiar with the popular online marketing software system. Small businesses can use Constant Contact to send out professional e-mail newsletters, conduct online surveys, and promote their events. The company's pitch to venture capitalists included the famous *New Yorker* cartoon of a dog sitting in front of a computer, telling another dog, "On the Internet, nobody knows you're a dog." "The company was founded with a pretty crisp passion," says Goodman, "which was making small businesses look great on the Internet."

Goodman is not a founder. She became CEO in 1999, and under her leadership, Constant Contact grew to more than 400,000 customers worldwide. She presided over an initial public offering in October 2007, when common shares of Constant Contact began trading on the Nasdaq Global Market. Soon after that, Constant Contact was named "Best Overall Company" at the 2009 American Business Awards.

What brand traits did Goodman leverage to build a great company? One of them was a passion for learning. Goodman graduated from the University of Pennsylvania and then received her MBA at Dartmouth. She was the daughter of an immigrant who became a chemist and wanted his children to be educated so they could do even better. Goodman's two brothers went to Yale, and she calls herself the "black sheep underachiever." She says, "I have a wildly successful family. But that's a story for a beer." She laughs.

FROM YOUR BRAND TO PROFITABILITY

How does Goodman's brand drive top-line growth and profitability? She's infused this passion for learning into the culture. And that has been a differentiator, especially in a technology company in a fast-changing industry. "One of the things we got right, and I'll take some modest credit for it, is we knew we were not our customer," she says. "We [had to learn about them]. We couldn't assume we knew what they needed—we had to ask them."

The focus on learning helped the company evolve. People at the company thought about everything. They attracted people who resonated with that culture. When they decided to stop thinking of the organization as just a software company, they had to base its identity on customer research. They began building customer ease into everything the company did—from easy use to hints, tips, webinars, and newsletters—to make life easier for its customers.

This relentless focus on learning drove real value. It also saved the company from going under. In 2003, spam hit cyberspace like a tidal wave. It was a huge threat, as Internet service providers (ISPs) started trying to block spam. Spammers were preventing Constant Contact customers from sending legitimate e-mail. Goodman starting boning up, invited her two biggest competitors to form a trade association, wrote white papers, and contacted legislators.

Since they soon knew more than policy makers, the group got legislation passed that led to the CAN-SPAM Act of 2003, making what spammers did illegal while protecting legitimate marketers. Learning triumphed. It remains a leadership value at Constant Contact. "I personally use peer mentoring, read books, and have a coach," says Goodman. "We are all learners, all the time."

This relentless focus on learning has made Constant Contact a more valuable resource to customers who have signed long-term contracts, and who keep using the service today.

Achieving Spectacular Results

As you trace back how your brand drives value, you should also be able to connect values to actions and results. The values help your company to overcome obstacles, drive results, and achieve goals. How can you make sure this happen all the time?

From Brand Value to Results

Imagine that an important value, an essential part of your brand, is persistence—never giving up. Maybe you came by this value when you were young. Perhaps, the story goes, you played the sax, joined the high school band, lost interest, and wanted to quit, but your parents insisted you stick it out. As you stayed on in the band, you became a very good musician. The longer you were there, the more friendships you found there. You became one of the best and received an award for excellence; later you went on to play in a jazz band in college and found a profound sense of satisfaction and accomplishment. That experience taught you the value of persistence. It is now core to your brand.

Now let's imagine that you have been leading your team through a challenging time. They've been working on a big deal for months. Now they've learned that they're on the brink of losing the business. The prospect has invited another company do an initial assessment, which could lead to securing the contract. Your team members are discouraged, dismayed, and ready to give up.

You want to remind them of the importance of never giving up. You believe deep down that they don't really want to quit. They need some one to remind them that digging deep and giving it your all is one of the secrets to success. You share that story—and remind them of that value of persistence. They are inspired. They now know they will never attain the satisfaction of winning if they quit now.

Exercise

Perhaps that hypothetical story and the way it's applied to a current situation has inspired you to think about one of your own experiences. It's time to think about one of these experiences and connect the value to a result that you've achieved. There are only two questions in this exercise, but they are powerful. When you do this, you'll see the connection between communicating your brand values and what is happening in your organization.

YOUR EXERCISE: BRAND-TO-RESULTS

Write about a time, as in the story above, when you saw that people needed to act on a value that was key to their success.

_____

_____

_____

_____

_____

How did you communicate this value to drive a result? What was the outcome, and how would you measure it?

_____

_____

_____

_____

_____

_____

_____

Think about the impact of communicating your values in story form. Perhaps you remember as a result that you completed a project, landed a new client, or saved money, or managed through a difficult crisis.

Once you see the power of this, you'll always want to share your values through stories. You will make a conscious effort to talk about your values in story form. By thoughtfully communicating the brand value, you'll witness how it goes to work your business, helping everyone find a path to success.

You'll also see how leveraging your values shape the culture. "We hire on culture and fire on culture," says Gail Goodman. "We are not shy about helping people who don't belong here to find an alternative career route." This doesn't mean that the company is "quick on the trigger," because it believes in trying to make people successful, but it also recognizes when there isn't a match. "That's always culture, not skills," says the CEO. "We can teach skills. It's always, always culture."

REAL-TIME CHALLENGE

Let's turn our attention to a current challenge. Are you facing an obstacle or difficult situation in your business? The core leadership beliefs and values that helped you prevail in the past will help you do so again. You can draw on your experiences and the lessons you've learned to help other people see a path to success.

Perhaps things are not going so well on a project; perhaps you are feeling competitive pressure, you've lost business, sales are off, or you've failed to meet a deadline. Maybe a major system has crashed or you've lost a key member of your team. Your team is feeling frustrated or angry.

It's time to draw on those leader brand values. Dig deep, and recall what got you here. Remember a time when you faced a similar challenge. This exercise should help you recall what worked before and communicate a solution or approach that will work.

REAL-TIME CHALLENGE EXERCISE

Name a situation that is frustrating you or challenging your team, one that is very difficult to resolve.

_____

_____

_____

What is this like? How is this similar to a challenge you successfully resolved in the past?

_____

_____

_____

What is the value and message you want to convey to your team?

_____

_____

_____

_____

REAL-TIME CHALLENGE EXAMPLE

Let's imagine a scenario that might help you make the most of this exercise. Imagine that you recently discovered a surprise cost overrun on a significant project that you thought was on track and on budget. You are really upset. You're ready to pounce on someone. You thought that appropriate measures were in place. It seems that several people weren't communicating. Now they are blaming each other.

You stop and think about a time when you've been here before. Once, it was *you* who was in a finger-pointing dispute. You vehemently disagreed about a course of action, the situation fell apart, and suddenly you were both in the boss's office. But you decided in that moment that blaming others wasn't what you were all about. In front of your boss, you took full responsibility. After some discussion, the issue was remedied. The person you were at odds with then appreciated the fact that you took ownership. He admitted to you that he had also acted badly and went back to your boss to share the whole story. As a result, you repaired your relationship. You became close colleagues; in fact, you became a great team. You learned from that experience how important it was to swallow your pride.

Now by sharing this story, you will be able to highlight a behavior that's important to *your* team's success. You will be able to convey to them in persuasive terms how important teamwork and cooperation are to your organization's success. By telling the story, you will have their attention and the message will be unmistakable. Everybody will get the point. You will have inspired your team. Your story will have inspired them and created a new framework for how they should behave.

What is that worth to the company? One powerful story that illustrates a value that drives your success changes the outcome and creates a measurable result. That is the power of communicating and leveraging your brand values.

WHY PEOPLE BELIEVE IN YOU

When you tell stories about your experiences, you illustrate how you authentically came to embrace certain values. Authenticity is so important to being a strong leader with a powerful brand. When people hear these stories, they know what you say is real. Your story brings a brand value into focus in a genuine way and makes it relevant. When you do this consistently, you change behaviors and drive values into the enterprise. If you are still not certain about the values that define your leadership, go back to the previous chapters, write and analyze your stories, and determine what they are telling you about your leadership brand.

Look at your life and career as a rich source of wisdom and strength for others. Understand what your stories say about your leadership, and share them. When challenges arise, look for opportunities to share the examples that provide context and meaning.

COMMUNICATING—YOUR BRAND VALUES

I have a client who was transferred to a division of her company at a time when they were struggling. Several legacy contracts with a major customer were in jeopardy. The technology had grown obsolete. The division needed to develop a new market for its product, and it saw the international market as the best opportunity.

The organization, however, had grown complacent over the years. The relationship-building muscle of the company had atrophied. They had grown reliant on long-time customers. They needed to take massive action, to get out and connect with international buyers as influential people in the United States who could facilitate introductions and meetings.

Recognizing this missing link in building relationships, my client asked her communications team to prepare a weekly e-mail. Each week, she began to share stories about her meetings with new prospects, at conferences and industry events where she brought key members of her team. She also highlighted stories from earlier years, when times were good, and sought out long-time employees who could highlight stories about how the organization built relationships years ago.

The theme that emerged was how important it was to listen to customers, understand their needs, and build trust. They had done it before, and if they could do it again, they had a chance at landing several new lucrative engagements. Her commitment to communicate the message made it stick. Morale improved. People started to take action. They moved from complacency to commitment. As a result, they were in line to win these engagements and believed that the relationships they were building would lead to other new contracts.

What this story illustrates is how the right leader communicating the right value can make a measurable impact. It wasn't as if no one in the organization was committed to building relationships in the past. The practice had gone dormant because it had not been communicated and reinforced. The leader, my client, reignited passion for client care, by modeling the behavior and expecting her team to listen to the customer. The more she wrote about it in her weekly e-mails, the more the organization began to appreciate and embrace its importance.

CHAPTER SUMMARY

- Leaders rise not only because of skill but also because of their reputations.
- Leverage your reputation to drive spectacular business results.
- You can carry your brand with you, into each organization you lead.
- Be true to the values that define you as a leader, and communicate them.
- Look for opportunities to share lessons through authentic personal stories.
- People are inspired to act by leaders who communicate brand values.

6

Personal Choices That Burnish Your Reputation

Goodwill is the only asset that competition cannot

undersell or destroy.

—MARSHALL FIELD

A REPUTATION, OR BRAND, IS A PROMISE. That promise has intrinsic value. When you honor the promise of your reputation, people learn to count on that. They learn they can expect you to act in ways that are consistent with that brand. This makes your brand reliable and that creates value. Every day you make choices about consistently living your brand. When you make good choices, it creates goodwill and builds trust. Building a brand is just like building a house. You do it brick by brick, choice by choice.

I asked many leaders who I interviewed for this book about difficult choices they had to make. Some of them were quite candid about mistakes they made. We're all human. Sometimes we may think we're doing the right thing and realize later that we didn't act consistently with our values. But every day we have another opportunity to make choices consistent with the leader we want to be.

I don't know anyone who hasn't made mistakes they regret. In the dark of night, we look back and wish we'd known what we know now. Perhaps we did what was expedient; perhaps we were hasty and didn't stop to think about the consequences, or perhaps we thought at the time that we didn't have a choice. Sometimes we ignore issues because it is easier, until we are forced to confront them and make a decision consistent with our values. Every day, we live and learn.

This chapter is about making choices that are consistent with your leadership brand values. I'll offer examples—real life choices—that have helped leaders burnish their brands. You'll find questions and exercises that will help you consider how to consistently make choices aligned with your brand values.

AL GOLIN, FOUNDER, GOLIN HARRIS

Al Golin began his public relations career as a field press representative with MGM Studios. He then joined the firm Max Cooper and Associates, with a staff of six, in 1956. At that time public relations was what most people referred to as "publicity" people. In 1957, Golin placed a cold call to Ray Croc, founder of the then-fledgling McDonald's hamburger chain. Kroc asked Golin to come over and meet him. An hour later, Golin started working for McDonald's on a retainer of $500 a month. McDonald's has been an account of Golin Harris for more than 50 years.

I asked Golin to reflect back on why he was able to forge such a strong, enduring relationship with Kroc. "I was very interested," he says. "I wanted to hear him out, what his vision was for this fledgling 15-cent hamburger thing he was starting, and how I could help him." Golin didn't just ask about the business; he wanted to understand Kroc's philosophy. "I knew he was the quintessential salesman," says Golin, "which made him a very good businessman. I've seen a lot of CEOs who have come from a financial or legal background, and they have no sales experience. It makes a big difference; they know that without a customer you have no business."

The Choices That Built the Brand

Golin is a curious guy. He's been good at asking questions, and perhaps even better at listening. During the meeting, Kroc did the talking. He wanted to attract franchisees. He needed Golin to put McDonald's on the map, but he didn't have an advertising budget. So Golin came up with an ingenious idea to help Kroc tell a story that would interest *real estate* people, who were the key to locating the growing chain of restaurants.

"I think Ray saw in me someone who was curious, creative, and saw beyond the obvious," Golin reflects. "My favorite word is *curiosity*. That's the keyword. In life and in our business, we have to be probing and curious and wanting to explore what's coming on the horizon." Golin admits curiosity is a trait he's exhibited since he was a kid. Today, it's essential to Golin Harris's brand, and it's also something Golin encourages in his grandkids. "I never like it when I see them not asking questions or not being interested," he says. Curiosity is an essential quality for most successful businesspeople.

Choosing to Hire People Who Represent Your Brand

How did this brand get "baked in" to the cake that is Golin Harris today? It was also choices about people. Golin emphasizes that "I always looked for people who embody those traits" of being probing and curious. He says that people created the chemistry that allowed the firm to grow. It is now 700 strong. A client as long term as McDonald's is unheard of in the PR world, where agencies are summarily hired and fired. "They like the kind of people we are," he says. "Chemistry will be the tie breaker, all things being equal. It doesn't replace being smart or creative, but it does make the client relationship work."

> "I wanted to work with people that I liked personally. And I think because if I liked them and enjoyed having a beer or lunch with them, then all things being equal, the chemistry was very important, not only in my relationship with them but in their relationship with clients."

As leaders we know that it is tempting to hire people who have a great résumé, especially when we are growing and need someone in a position.

However, at Golin Harris, hiring for this trait of curiosity has not been not optional; choosing people who represent the brand has been essential to its success. That is what has made Al Golin successful. It's always tempting to make an exception to fill a position. But when you are clear about building a brand that is aligned with important values, you'll wait to hire until you have that perfect brand fit.

Choosing to Back People Up

"We had a large account that we fought to get for six months; it was very competitive," recalls Golin. The company won the business, but immediately there was trouble. The individual managing the relationship for the client was making the agency's people miserable. Golin Harris raised the issue. "We told her diplomatically that this was not a way to treat people," says Golin. "We tried to explain that she wasn't going to get more out of them with that attitude." It continued, so Golin Harris resigned the account.

Golin notes that "it shocked her, she couldn't believe it. We told her our people are as important to us as you are." The message went out that the company had taken this dramatic step. "That was worth everything," he says. "I think even those who were more cynical became believers that we were a certain kind of company that would stick to its principles, even if it meant giving up revenue."

The word spread around the industry, and it generated a lot of buzz. Golin Harris was the kind of place where you wanted to work. The company began attracting talent it might not have seen otherwise. "It was a very important statement to make," says Golin.

KIP HOLLISTER, CEO, HOLLISTER

Kip Hollister grew up in Burlington, Vermont, daughter of a minister, and the fourth of five children. Today she is the founder and CEO of Hollister, a full-service staffing firm with a network of 15,000 businesses and 60,000 individuals. Early in life, Kip Hollister thought she would be a therapist. She received a degree in sociology with a minor in psychology. "I was all about self-improvement, self-introspection, listening, and caring for other people, so it was that or social work," she recalls.

After college, however, she found herself an opportunity in sales in a personnel firm. She discovered in herself an uncanny ability to sell. "At a very young age I learned that I could sell my way into a job, show them my work ethic, get myself trained, and overcome objections," she says. "Anything was possible."

Eventually she moved into recruiting. She soon learned she loved the work but hated how her boss treated people. Hollister notes that "morale was awful. I woke up one morning and said, 'I love, love, love what I do but don't respect where I am doing it.'" She thought, "I can get out of the industry or stay in it and run it the way I want to run it." At the time, she was 26. Too young to be scared, she sketched her business plan on a paper napkin and went out to hunt for office space. She hired one "rookie" and then another, to train them "from scratch." They came with open minds. "The vision I painted was: we are here to make a difference for people," she says.

Choosing to Listen

Breaking away from the stereotypical recruiting agency was difficult, and Hollister did it all. She was coach and player, touching every deal, a self-admitted "control freak." She says, "I masked my fears and anxiety by showing them how to do the job myself." Building the culture in the beginning was easy. "It was contagious," she observes, "I had instant followers. I got to set the pace and create the brand. I was just being me." The agency grew by leaps and bounds. Employees lived on hard work and passion.

At age 26, Hollister had to confront the fact that she hadn't been prepared for the challenge of managing a growing staff. Driven to succeed, stressed and frustrated, she urged people to hit the phones harder. "I was really angry," she recalls, "when they weren't at the highest level, I would rev myself up and scare them."

It took an employee, one of her first hires, to confront her with her behavior. Her frustration was having the opposite of the intended impact. Hollister recalls that "I took in that feedback. And I met with all of them. I was open to feedback, and I started forming culture in partnership with staff, instead of feeling like I had to have all the answers. That was a real shift for me."

"I took in that feedback. And I met with all of them. I was open to feedback, and I started forming culture in partnership with staff, instead of feeling like I had to have all the answers. That was a real shift for me."

Hollister credits her family upbringing for helping her accept tough feedback. Family dinners growing up had been a time for "fellowship and learning." She says, "I could push back on my dad, and he never got angry. He wanted to seek to understand." He was modeling the behavior.

"As a leader," she remarks, "I have chosen, for better or worse, to be transparent during the highs and lows." The company has survived and ultimately thrived after three recessions. "When times are great, I share what's going great and why; but when times are tough, I also share," she explains.

Choosing to Be Transparent

Hollister says this experience led her to make another choice: to be transparent, even in difficult times. She does this even "when times are tough, which is a humble time—you're not at the top of your game." Transparency is part of her brand; she believes in it as the vehicle for building trust. "Ultimately that builds your culture. You can trust that through thick or thin," she says, "they'll know what is real and where you stand."

In the spirit of open communication, the Hollister staffing office floor is wide open, with no doors. The staff has a lot of brown-bag lunches. This experience is new for many people. Once, she asked staff members to raise their hands if they grew up in a family where there was good communication. Only 20 percent raised their hands. "I knew that it would be a value I would have to show by the way I behaved each day," observes Hollister, "pushing people out of their comfort zone to adopt it."

Kip Hollister is so committed to this open style that she hired a consultant to facilitate brown-bag meetings, to be sure she hears the message straight. The result? In an industry notorious for high employee turnover, Hollister retains top people.

Transparency is a word that is often used in business and leadership; however, in my experience as a coach, transparency seems to be rarely practiced to a sufficient degree. Kip Hollister has chosen to live by the value and hold herself accountable to it. That choice to go the extra mile to adhere to your values makes a powerful statement to your team.

CHOICES THAT BURNISH YOUR BRAND

Where is your company out of alignment with important values that are part of your brand?

_____

_____

Do you have a difficult choice to make?

_____

_____

If so, what needs to be done?

_____

_____

Where can you get the support you need to make that happen?

_____

_____

When will you do this?

_____

_____

Choosing to Let Go

Every leader faces challenges in deciding whether to keep people on the team when they are contributors but not aligned with company values. Often we have people we regard as "high performers," but they don't practice the values that are important to the organization's success. "I had a leadership team in place, and some of them would just 'yes' me," says Kip Hollister. "Then when the recession hit, there was an implosion." Hollister worked with a consultant who warned her that some of her leaders were not acting in ways that were consistent with their value system. She chose to ignore it when the company was going full steam. Yet things kept getting worse.

"Four months later, I called [the consultant] and said, okay, I want to do work on this," she recalls. Still fearful about letting go of "top performers," she told the consultant it was a difficult decision, but one she knew she had to make. "They were driving business results, but they were not aligned with culture and values, and guess what? You have a dysfunctional culture as a result."

The first thing she did was to work with the consultant to clearly define the culture. They transformed it into a working document that declared who the company was and what it stood for. "Once you have that in place, everything is easy," she says, "because you are able to attract the talent. You can share your story and hire against that." Recruiting outstanding talent who also represented her brand was a matter of making an unwavering commitment. Hollister notes that "once you make the decision, they come."

"You have to have your own strong personal leadership brand," observes Hollister, "because brand is built from the inside out." Your brand doesn't mean much if you don't build the culture internally. "You will be found out, you will be a phony, and it will not be authentic," says Hollister.

Choosing to Create a Culture

As a company grows, it becomes more important than ever to nurture and stay true to that brand. Doing so is especially challenging for entrepreneurs, who started their companies "from scratch." While your brand values have shaped the company, those values have to live in the organization.

Kip Hollister started to recognize she had to move the organization away from being "Kip-centric" to being "brand-centric." She says: "Even though it is my personal brand, with my values of integrity, passion, and open communication, [I'm always asking myself,] how do I build a firm and a culture that supports that and takes me out of it?

"It all goes back to [having] the right people on the bus. Once you have the right people on the bus, it's about incorporating them in a collaborative way into what we want to be about."

MATT DAVIS, THE DOW CHEMICAL COMPANY—ON MOVING INTO A LEADERSHIP ROLE

As Senior Vice President of Global Public Affairs at The Dow Chemical Company, Matt Davis today sits on the executive committee and reports directly to the CEO of Dow. He's not only a leader, he has had the opportunity to mentor dozens of other leaders. Matt is passionate about how important it is to discover and build your personal brand and be conscious of how you want to lead.

"I started in public affairs in 1986 as an intern at Dow. I kept getting roles I liked," he recalls. He set his sights on becoming the vice president of Public Affairs. It took a long time. "The day before I addressed the organization for the first time as a leader was an emotional time for me," he says. "I'd been given the role I'd wanted for 23 years, and suddenly thought, what am I going to do with it?"

A mentor told him, "Matt, you have to become the leader of this function. You have to allow other people to grow." This wise friend advised him to stop being the "doer" and start viewing things from the leader's vantage point—become the strategic voice of the function.

Choosing to Lead, Not Do

"It was tough, I'd been such a doer, and I had to reexamine how I saw myself," says Davis. "I had to become the motivator, inspiring people. I also had to focus on getting the right person into the right job."

> "I'd been such a doer, regionally, and I had to reexamine how I saw myself," says Davis. "I had to be the motivator, inspiring people, and focus on getting the right person into the right job."

Transitioning to being a leader who inspires and motivates others is perhaps the greatest challenge many face in moving into leadership roles. You have probably been there yourself. You know how to do it. You've proven that. But you have to put doing aside and learn to lead. "You don't have time to sit at your computer and do the tactical work," says Davis. "Yet, I see that at the very top of large companies. People get to that level because they turn out results, but then they get promoted and need to get things done through other leaders."

Davis successfully transitioned. Now, as a mentor to others, he advises them to step back and learn to effectively communicate. As energizing as it can be to get in there and get it done, when you're doing, you're not acting as a leader. Set the agenda, communicate the plan, align the organization, monitor results, hold people accountable, and inspire them to the highest level of performance.

As a coach I've watched new leaders crash and burn after a promotion for this very reason. If you find yourself in a similar situation, it's time to hit the Pause button. The choice to lead by communicating your values and insisting that your leaders do the same, is one of the most important you can make. "Now I run the function globally and think bigger picture," reflects Davis. It's a change in mindset. Then, you begin assessing which new skills you need to be an effective leader.

What are you "doing" that you need to let go of, so that you can lead?

1. _____

_____

_____

2. _____

_____

_____

3. _____

_____

_____

What steps will you take to let go of doing and start leading?

1. _____

_____

_____

2. _____

_____

_____

3. _____

_____

_____

Choosing to Learn New Skills

Another choice that Matt Davis had to make was to be tougher and more decisive. He has always been admired as an approachable, accessible person, with high energy and a strong presence. The feedback he received when he was promoted to the top job in the function was that he was "too nice." He knew it meant that he would have to make some changes without giving up an essential aspect of who he was.

In Matt's case, choosing what kind of leader to be meant developing a skill he had not previously needed. He learned to be more hard-line on decisions, to negotiate the disagreements and make the difficult calls. In a Fortune 100 company, his is a demanding job, which requires not only a strong work ethic but also the ability to make a decision and not waver. He discovered he could still be himself—the high-energy, accessible, approachable person. He just needed to add a new more decisive dimension to his leadership brand.

Many times when we move into new roles, we wonder whether we will have to "change." You are who you are. Your brand is your brand. You don't have to change, but you sometimes do have to add new skills. When you become aware of the need to develop these skills and work hard to acquire them, you are going to be successful. Matt says, "I realized that this transformation was essential for both the function and the company."

Still he vowed not to lose the fun. "Our employee surveys show workload and stress are the highest concern of employees. I want to remove those barriers, because in the business we are in, you are only creative if you are relaxed and energized."

Choosing a Healthy Life

The demands of leadership mean we have to take care of ourselves to perform at the top of our game. You can't do the job if you're not fit, physically and mentally. For many of us, this isn't easy. We know what to do. It's hard to do it.

Yet every leader's brand really needs to include vitality, strength, and vigor. As a leader, you have to exude presence, as well as passion, enthusiasm, and energy. If you don't put your health first, you're putting your life, career, and family at risk.

The biggest challenge most people have in choosing a healthy lifestyle is time. There are more demands than there are hours. If you find you are letting go of the workout, sleep, or time to get a healthy meal, you have to build these activities into your schedule.

If you are clear that energy, vitality, and health are your brand, getting clear about this brand is the first step. If you are not clear, then you will let it slide. Time management helps, but if you don't get clear, you won't do what you know you should do.

In the wee hours of the morning it's hard to get out of bed to go to the gym. For some people it's easier when you're traveling; for others, it's more difficult. Even if there is a great workout room at the hotel, you have a 7 a.m. meeting; you'll be going until 7 p.m., when you have dinner with a client. Whether you fly privately or commercially, you pack your schedule. Yet, you know that no matter where you are, you are going to have to "show up" as that energetic, vital leader. That means making time to maintain physical and emotional health.

In our 24/7 culture, you can work out, meditate, have a healthy breakfast. You can find 15 minutes to call your family or sit in your room and decompress. If you don't, you'll soon find yourself in a bad place. That's when anger, frustration, fear, anxiety, and other emotions can get the best of you.

Your physical and emotional life has an impact on everyone around you. None of us is perfect. We are emotional beings. It is difficult when we are stressed to manage the emotion. The best way to do it is to maintain a healthy lifestyle. Although I'm devoted to working out and eating right, I still find it challenging when I'm involved in a big project, traveling, or on a deadline. When you feel yourself falling "off the wagon," get through it, then reset, and recommit to taking care of yourself.

A respected leader I know had physically let himself go. He had gained a lot of weight over the years. He had trouble walking, breathing, and handling the demands of the job. His leadership image was suffering. He often wasn't taken seriously by others. Finally, he got fed up and lost over 80 pounds.

Today he dresses nicely, his energy level is different, and he has more self-confidence. Now people talk with him differently, treat him differently, and see him differently. His physical form has given him tremendous confidence. He's asserting himself, he doesn't mind being in front of people, and he's therefore more visible and making a far greater impact.

Choosing Emotional Health

The choice to be mindful about your emotional life is just as important. "There are days when I come to the office and have to talk myself up," says Matt Davis. "I can't be down, because if I am frowning, kicking the trash can, or having emotional outbursts, people think something is wrong, and they get uptight."

There is room for emotion in business. No one is perfect. A healthy amount of frustration expressed appropriately will get people's attention. But it becomes a "brand killer" if you always carry around anger or frustration. We've worked with many executives in this situation. Their frustration leads to outbursts or interactions they regret. If it becomes a pattern, it damages your leader brand.

Leaders tend to believe they are superhuman. They keep pushing themselves. Hard work is hardwired into you. You may not realize that you are overcome by work, stressed or suffering from a lack of personal time. If you feel physically or emotionally depleted, that's a warning sign.

HEALTHY LEADER BRAND CHECKLIST

If you find yourself feeling frustrated, angry, depressed, upset, or anxious on a regular basis, it's time to take action.

Chances are you need to stop and take care of yourself.

What can you do to restore your physical and emotional health, and maintain your energetic, vital leader brand?

- Decide health is your "brand."
- Put healthy activity on your calendar.
- Be ruthless about this priority.
- Eliminate unnecessary tasks.
- Exercise several times a week.
- Consider meditation and yoga.
- Choose healthy food.
- Carve out personal time.
- Spend time with friends.
- Make family time a high priority.
- Connect often with people you like.
- Read and stimulate your mind.
- Enjoy sports, theater, and movies.
- Listen to music and go to concerts.
- Take in the sights where you travel.
- Schedule vacations before all else.
- Have a spontaneous getaway.
- Let others know that this effort is important.
- Ask your assistant to protect time.
- Put white space on your calendar.
- Give yourself time to think and reflect.
- Encourage your team to be healthy.
- Make health part of your culture.
- Put more fun in your life.

Perhaps you have not handled things at work the way you wanted to. Perhaps you are acting out in stressful ways at home. You are talking about work all the time. Or you are simply so preoccupied that you can't enjoy the time with family and friends.

At that point you have to recognize that your equilibrium is off. It's time to reclaim it! Do some of the things listed in the sidebar, or whatever helps you regain a sense of health and well-being.

You are the only person who can make sure you are taking care of you. Nothing is worth risking your health and the relationships important to you. Your children, spouse, friends, and colleagues need you. Do it for yourself and for them.

CHOOSING YOUR GAME FACE

So, you're taking good care of yourself. There still will be days when you have to rally and put on your game face. When I worked in television, I had a lot of practice with this. Every single morning at 5 a.m. no matter how I felt, that camera light went on, the opening music played, and the morning show began. It was great practice for putting on my game face. I wouldn't be successful on television if I couldn't put aside whatever was on my mind and focus on being the best I could be.

Putting on your game face is a skill, and you can learn how to do it. It's important, because people are always watching. They assume that if you're in a bad mood, it is their fault. Once again, we've all been there. I don't know many people who ace this aspect of leadership; however, you feel better, and your team feels better, if you can learn the discipline of regaining your equilibrium before you walk in the door.

Smiling actually changes your mood. Don't beat yourself up if you don't do it every single day. Just strive to learn how to manage your emotion this way. And, don't let it get to you! If you're having a tough time with certain people, give yourself permission to ignore the critics and troublemakers. There's always going to be a problem, and there's always going to be a crisis. Believe it will work out, put on your game face, and find something to laugh about.

If you feel things are starting to get to you, one way to handle them is to leave the office. Take a walk, go to lunch, do something different. Take yourself out of that space for a while. When you have a major task to focus on, work from home. Do something radical. Take a whole weekend off—yes, a *whole* weekend. Tell people you won't be reachable. Have your assistant handle calls and e-mail. When you return, you'll be charged up, energized, enthusiastic, confident, and ready to tackle the issues.

You also need friends. I've seen many leaders derail because they didn't have friends, colleagues, mentors, coaches, or trusted advisors whom they could call on. Isolation can distort your view. Having people to turn to, not just in crisis, but all the time, is one of the most important things you can do for your emotional and psychological health. If you have friends, colleagues, and associates you enjoy but haven't connected with in a while, make it a point to do so.

CHOOSING A POLISHED PROFESSIONAL IMAGE

The topic of image will not be covered in detail in this book. However, image is very important way to communicate nonverbally in a way that is consistent with your leadership brand values. Image is a brand reinforcement, a way of outwardly reflecting the leader you are on the inside. Wardrobe, grooming, even the state of your office are signals about the inner you; who you are and what you stand for.

As a leader, if you don't know how to dress, your look is out of sync with your brand. There is no escaping the fact that image matters. We are conditioned as human beings to notice whether someone "fits in" or "stands out," and if the signal is out of sync with the individual's position, we tend to believe what we see. Likewise, if the state of your office is out of sync with the leader you want to be, then people are confused and tend to actually believe what they see, not what you say.

Managing your professional image and surroundings isn't difficult if you learn how to do it from the pros and take steps to make sure that your image and surroundings are always consistent with what you want to communicate. It doesn't matter whether or not you like to shop, or clean, or organize. You can find people to help you develop your style, get help choosing clothing that represents your brand, and keeping your office in order. You can learn the skills of managing your wardrobe and your surroundings. There isn't any excuse for not having the wardrobe, grooming, and office surroundings that project the leader you are.

I've sent many clients to our wardrobe consultant (Mary Lou Andre with Organization by Design) and realized the issue wasn't about the clothes. It was about getting their life organized, having the clothes they needed for all parts of their life, and being prepared for every situation. And, perhaps more powerfully, it wasn't just about how they looked, but about how they felt. Looking great and keeping your surroundings clean, orderly, and comfortable gives you confidence. You stride into the room. You enjoy working in your office. Like physical health, wardrobe, grooming, presence and style have to be part of your brand.

Professional dress is an important part of your leadership brand, so it's important to put time and energy into getting it just right. If you haven't had professional coaching or image consulting, do yourself a favor and find someone who is really good to help you out. If you need someone to come in and show you how to file, organize, and keep an executive office, it is well worth the investment.

Make sure that that anyone who works with you understands the demands of your job, what is expected in your profession, and how others dress and keep their offices. Professional dress is not about fashion although it is important to be on trend, to demonstrate that you are current. When choosing a consultant, look at how he or she dresses as your first clue as to whether they can help you. Some image consultants are not qualified to work with corporate leaders, and if you can't find the right person, go to a store where you can buy quality clothing and try out a few associates until you find one who is helpful, not pushy—who listens, knows the merchandise, and is really there to help you be your best.

IMAGE CASE STUDY NO. 1

One of our clients, the chief financial officer (CFO) of a large company was in line to become chief executive officer (CEO) in the next two years. He had worked hard to improve his presentations to the board, but he also received feedback that he needed to step up his image, to "look" like a CEO. He worked in a casual environment. He liked to be "comfortable." But his wardrobe wasn't doing him any favors. His suits were old, his ties were too conservative, and his shirts didn't fit.

After he worked with our image consultant, the results were amazing. He threw out the clothing that didn't match his leader brand. He purchased beautiful suits and casual business attire that made him look like the next CEO. They were beautifully tailored and allowed him to stand out while fitting in perfectly with executives in his industry. He had the right wardrobe for events like conferences and golf outings.

He looked and felt like he was on top of the world. It paid off in spades. The board, clients, and other executives were commenting positively. There were no longer any questions about whether he was ready for the corner office.

Choosing the Brand Image for Your Office

Some of us do not have the luxury of choosing the décor for our office and surroundings. Nevertheless, once you get to a level of leadership, you should be able to exert some control. Whether you inherit your furnishings, or whether you can decorate yourself, think about what kind of image you want to project. This is a very important part of your brand.

The office image has to be aligned with the culture and vibe of your company. Within those parameters you can give it your personal touch. If you aren't sure how to do it, there are plenty of excellent corporate design experts to help you.

I believe in making your office personal, but not too personal. A few photographs are great. A wall of them can make people wonder what you're thinking about at work. That isn't to say that you shouldn't be a family person, or display your hobbies, or have a theme. This is a very personal space as well as a professional one. You should enjoy being there, and it should make you happy. You spend a lot of time in the office.

IMAGE CASE STUDY NO. 2

Another client, a woman who was the president of a division, had come from an IT background, where the dress was always casual in the office and even vendors and others she met were dressed down. Over the years, she had collected a few suits for major events like her global presentations or board meetings, but she rarely updated these, and most of the time she dressed too casually in the office. One day, she had a business event at her house, and when she walked down the stairs, someone who hadn't met her was surprised to learn that she was the chief information officer.

This was the catalyst for a conversation about her wardrobe and style that was difficult but necessary. She was traveling constantly, didn't have that much interest in clothing, and though she had the money to invest, had never investigated the right resources. Once again, we set her up with a wardrobe consultant as well as a department store where they provided excellent service and assistance. Because of that, when clothing she purchased needed to be tailored or shipped, or when she needed accessories, the store had her size, the consultant knew what was in her wardrobe, and they could coordinate her wardrobe for events or travel as needed without taking a lot of her time.

Her transformation was equally impressive. She discovered that she could be comfortable and also dressed like an executive when she chose quality, good fit, and color and style that flattered her and allowed her to stand out while fitting in perfectly with other executives. While she was just a little concerned about how her own team would perceive this transformation, they were very complimentary. What she learned is that people want you to show up looking, acting, and sounding like a leader, and the way you dress is part of that.

I am always amazed at the clutter in some people's offices. I rarely see that with a CEO. Most CEOs have arrived there because they know how to manage time, paper, projects, and space. If you have not mastered this part of your life, now is the time to bring in an organizational expert. One common issue when people have too much clutter is they don't have the right place to put materials. So build in what you need, and consider going more paperless. Let your assistant help you get it under control and keep it under control. Many leaders have been passed over for promotion simply because they don't seem to have it under control. Peek into their offices? You know!

In the next chapter, we'll move on to look at the most effective ways to communicate your leadership brand.

CHAPTER SUMMARY

- Your brand image is shaped every day by the personal choices you make.
- Those choices include how you decide to show up as a leader.
- They also include how you hire and treat the people who work for you.
- Take care of your emotional and physical health, as they are vital to your brand.
- Image is an important part of leadership brand, reflecting the leader on the inside.

Communicate Your Leadership Brand

*A brand is a living entity—and it is enriched
or undermined cumulatively over time, the
product of a thousand small gestures.*

—MICHAEL EISNER, CEO DISNEY

IN 2003, FRED COOK BECAME THE
third CEO of Colin Harris in 54 years, when Al Colin stepped aside.
As the baton was passed, the financial picture at Golin Harris was a bit
shaky. "We had grown complacent," recalls Cook. "We were resting on
our laurels. A collaborative, friendly, and supportive culture meant that
after we lost a new business pitch, you'd see a flurry of e-mails congratulat-
ing everybody for coming in second or third. We were talking about how
hard we had worked. That wasn't what I wanted."

Cook faced a dilemma. How could he infuse a winning attitude, part
of his brand, without losing what had worked at Golin Harris? He thought,
first, that people had to *think* of themselves as winners or as "nice guys
that would kick your ass." He wanted to turn up the heat and change the
chemistry of the company without changing the people.

Think about a time when you've faced a similar situation. You looked
around and realized that you had good people. They were capable of doing
the job. But something wasn't working. How did you preserve the best of

the culture while also instilling new values that would help you attain better results? The first thing Cook did was to celebrate and reward what he wanted to emphasize—a winning attitude. "If a team won a piece of business, I sent out trophies with the Golin Harris logo. They came with a note card from me along with a gift card for $50." These were tangible reminders of the values that Cook wanted to drive home.

Next, Cook started measuring success. That may sound like a no-brainer, but as a coach, I'm constantly surprised at how companies aren't tracking the behaviors and actions they want to encourage. Golin Harris started tracking "winning" success every way they could measure it, and by 2007, four short years later, they had won Agency of the Year awards from three different organizations. "It was a grand slam, the culmination of our turnaround," recalls Cook. "We were back."

The next and sometimes more difficult challenge is to sustain the momentum. Once you establish a new way of doing things, how do you keep it going? It is easy for people to fall back on behaviors that are familiar. Here's what Cook says they did at Golin Harris: "We got reprints from *PR Week* and reprinted the article for every employee. Al and I signed one for each of our 700 employees." One of the trophies was mailed from office to office, to all 30 around the globe. People were encouraged to send back videos of the trophy. "They had it in front of the Eiffel Tower, on a ferry boat in Hong Kong, people were sleeping with it, kissing it," recalls Cook, "and we shared all this on our website. Everybody could check in and see the photographs."

The result was that it stuck. Within a few years, the company was thriving financially. "What I am most proud of is we went from almost no profit to better than 20 percent margin without changing any of the senior management team," says Cook. Golin Harris preserved what worked, while infusing a new value, by highlighting the value and making the message stick. People were excited because they were part of a winning team.

"What I am most proud of is we went from almost no profit to better than 20 percent margin without changing any of the senior management team," says Cook.

HOW TO COMMUNICATE WHEN STARTING A NEW ROLE

Cook wasn't well known to the Golin Harris leadership team when he was brought from Los Angeles to Chicago and then made CEO a few short months later. "Suddenly I was moving from being a peer to their boss," recalls Cook, "and I think for anybody that can be a challenging experience." He sensed the difficulty many people had: "It is one thing to be given a title and another to earn the respect that comes with the title."

Cook did what any smart leader would do. He sat down and talked with each leader, one-on-one. "I wanted to understand their strengths and leverage them," he says. "Then it was a matter of convincing them the change was good for the company."

This endeavor built momentum for a course of action. People saw that he was serious and made decisions to embrace those values. You can't drive brand value if everyone on your team isn't aligned. Having just one person who is not committed can sink the ship. You have to ask for, and receive, 100 percent commitment. As you start in a new role, ask people to come with you, demonstrate you are serious, get them on board, and consistently communicate your expectations.

CREATING A COMMUNICATION STRATEGY TO SUPPORT BRAND VALUES

Once everyone is on board, it's time to cascade the message with a communication plan. Driving change and incorporating new values takes a sustained effort. People need to hear the message many times. You have to connect logically and emotionally. That's what people at Golin Harris did by celebrating success. They connected the idea with an emotion. Winners were high-fiving and smiling when they got their awards.

Setting up the plan and then communicating regularly is the key to success. For people at Golin Harris, this effort wouldn't have worked had they stopped after a few weeks or even months. They kept momentum and spirits high, so people began to see that the message really matters. They focused on winning.

A good communications strategy is necessary to coordinating and driving the internal messaging that shapes your brand. Without a plan, people to execute it, projects to promote it, and time and effort, the attempt will fail. One of the biggest mistakes organizations make is failing to communicate the values in creative ways over a sustained period of time.

If you wonder why change isn't happening fast enough in your organization, chances are it's a failure to communicate. Put that plan together. Then, put muscle behind it. This means daily, weekly, and monthly activities—and I don't mean people standing at the front of the room with PowerPoint slides. Be creative, be engaging, find ways to reach people, and be sure that your own team of leaders is doing the same.

The reason it is important to have a team of people who can communicate is clear. As the leader, you can shout it from the mountaintops, but in a large corporation, employees respond better to their own managers. That means that your plan to deliver the message has to be shared with your direct reports, and in turn to their direct reports, and they need to know how to communicate, motivate, inspire. Your entire team needs to consistently communicate the values in a way that engages others. A good communication plan in a large organization requires everyone in a leadership role to be involved, committed, and skilled. Many organizations with superb CEOs still have bottlenecks because those farther down in the organization don't have the skill and ability to cascade the message. Your executive team, their direct reports, managers, as well as functions, including human resources and communications teams, have to do their part. The best communication strategies that drive internal change involve every leader in the organization.

Sometimes, one ingenious idea can be the linchpin for the whole communications plan. For Golin Harris, that was the trophy. Employees were chattering about where it would pop up next. It became the topic of frequent water cooler conversation. Everybody got into the act and had fun with it. That's the kind of cleverness that makes a message stick. "When I walk around the office and look into people's cubicles, they still have those articles posted or framed," observes Cook. "The trophies are on their desks. It's a constant reminder that we are winners. People feel our company is going somewhere."

COMMUNICATING AS YOUR COMPANY GROWS

Gail Goodman, CEO of Constant Contact, has presided over explosive company growth. By 2011 the company had 400,000 customers and hundreds of employees in 20 locations. It was a far cry from the early days when almost everyone had attended a lunch with Goodman and they measured the size of the company by the number of pizzas they ordered. "I used to do 24 lunches a year, but we couldn't scale it," says Goodman. She had to take a new approach to making sure the brand values were promoted consistently.

> "I used to do 24 lunches a year, but we couldn't scale it," says Goodman.

Today, Constant Contact calls 30-minute company meetings every other week, which are broadcast in-house. "I help shape the topics," says Goodman, "but I'm not the sole speaker. I screen the agenda to make sure we talk about what needs to be talked about." Constant Contact has its own internal social network, which is an important tool for Goodman.

In addition, the company is committed to teaching leaders about the Constant Contact way. It has leadership development where the focus is to "make sure leaders understand who our customers are and the problem we're trying to solve." Goodman also holds "skip-level meetings" every six months with every direct report to her own direct reports. "They are the people now influencing the organization, so it's important that I know who they are and that they feel comfortable coming in my door," she explains.

CREATING A CULTURE OF COMMUNICATION

The bigger the company, the more important it becomes to create a culture of communication and train your people to be very good at it. That means everyone needs to embrace the idea that communication matters. They must learn to streamline the message, to make it crisp, clear, and memorable. They must know how to make every word count, and often count every word. "I'm a gigantic believer in simplicity," says Bob Kelly, CEO of BNY Mellon. "The one thing I can't stand is walking into a meeting and having somebody put me through a 40-slide deck."

When Kelly became CEO, he watched a parade of lengthy, meandering presentations, and then he told everyone to show up with only *one* summary slide. Imagine the shock that would go off in most organizations if people were told to do that! But that's what happened at BNY Mellon. Getting a presentation down to one slide (with a few back-up slides behind it) improved productivity and efficiency at that organization. Kelly believes it was also a leadership development tool. Leaders had to learn how to communicate without data dumping. If they hadn't taken time to analyze the data and make a compelling case, "it's an indication that they didn't understand the issue," says Kelly. "It means that you can't summarize their thoughts and get to the point."

What's the result? "In our last board meeting we had an executive talk to *one* slide in an engaging way," recalls Kelly. "He read the audience, knew what they wanted to hear, and I got feedback from the board that it was the best presentation they'd seen in 20 years."

PowerPoint doesn't have to be the "death" of communication when it is used well. It is not a bad tool. In fact, it's a good one, used poorly by most people. The reason we waste time and accomplish little isn't the technology; it is a failure to think and clarify before preparing the presentation. In creating a culture of communication, every leader needs ongoing support to learn a high level of skill in thinking and framing issues at the leadership level. Presenters need to learn to not just data dump, but to tell the story behind the data. They must know how to create meaning and context and also connect at the logical and emotional level. They must also understand how to prepare different types of presentations, from those for sales meetings, where they need to engage people, to those for board meetings, where they must inform and drive strategic decisions.

To that end, we at Bates Communications have developed a simple but powerful six-slide Template for Presentation to Decision Makers. The results executives have when they use this tool have been outstanding. In decision-making settings, our clients find it helps them to become more succinct and clear, and demonstrate they can think and speak at the strategic level. The secret to this and every type of presentation is to understand your audience and to think it through in advance. There are many more tips on how to do this in *Speak Like a CEO*, and my second book, *Motivate Like a CEO*.

"In our last board meeting we had an executive talk to *one* slide in an engaging way," recalls Kelly. "He read the audience, knew what they wanted to hear, and I got feedback from the board that it was the best presentation they'd seen in 20 years."

One important factor in every presentation is to analyze your audience and then focus on one big idea. Think about them. Write down what they want to know. Then create a presentation about them. Don't go into your "file" of slides and lift the same old stuff. Each audience is different. Make an effort to connect with them. Be interesting, be clever, and be engaging.

Bob Kelly is known as a confident, conversational, and informal presenter. It's his brand. Ask people in the organization about him—it's one of the first things they mention. Talk about a powerful brand! People admire his informal but engaging presence and his comfort with any audience. That has been a significant factor in his success.

The Value of Symbolism

People are listening but they're also watching. Symbolism matters. Kelly's predecessor spent a lot of time in his office. Kelly wanted to promote a different kind of culture, where senior leaders could be more connected, where they interacted and were collaborative. In the risky, highly regulated world of financial services, that goal is important. More leaders need to take ownership of decisions.

What did Kelly do to send the message? He says that "I started walking around unannounced, asking them, 'What's the deal on this? How are you thinking about that?'" The symbolism was clear. People had to share and take ownership of their areas. "You have to give responsibility and accountability to a lot more people," notes Kelly, "and of course create governance and metrics around that," he says, so people can't get too far off course.

Kelly also got rid of the rectangular conference room table adjoining his office, replacing it with a round table. "I didn't want 'Dad' at the head table making decisions. We were going to discuss things together. I was saying, 'This is no longer a hierarchy.' I didn't want people to suck up to me as a power broker. That's the last thing I wanted."

Most leaders responded well. Some did leave the company. "It is just a different way of operating, and it was hard for some people," says Kelly. "But in the end, if people can't make it, they can't make it. If you make simple changes quickly, it has an impact, in a short period of time."

Town Halls and Company Meetings

Bob Kelly travels about half of his time, and he sets up town hall meetings without agendas. "I just talk, no slides, then I answer any question," notes Kelly. He says he's just interested in hearing what people are thinking. The ability to stand in front of the room, especially at town hall and company meetings, is especially important to him.

For most large companies, town hall meetings and corporate events are important forums. You are investing a lot of time and money, and you might as well make it a memorable experience. At Bates Communications we have helped leaders with hundreds of these presentations. The best combine creativity and great platform performance with an interactive approach. The more you command the stage, engage the audience, and surprise, the better the message will stick.

Most leaders who handle town hall meetings well appreciate there is an element of showmanship to it. "My job is to entertain the group," says Kelly. "You need to get them comfortable and get them to listen to you, so they don't fall asleep!" If you are uncomfortable embracing the entertainment aspect, watch other leaders you admire. It has to be authentic.

Tell stories, use video, audience response, music, audience participation, and humor to liven things up. You don't have to be Jay Leno, but people remember what they feel, and laughter is one of the best ways to engage and make a message memorable. If you're just going to stand up and deliver a dry, bullet-point presentation, my advice is to send a memo. It's cheaper.

Many leaders really enjoy a question-and-answer session, and that's probably the simplest way to get people engaged. If you ask for questions and you're met with silence, start by asking the first question yourself, get people to jot down questions, or have them use technology. Today, you can actually leverage technology, for example, by telling people not to turn off the BlackBerrys and iPhones, and instead to text you a question while you're onstage. Be creative and let the audience know you're interested in them.

You need a team to create a great meeting, so my advice is recruit a good communications team, and tell them what you hope will come out of the meeting. Ask them to get creative and find ways to make it memorable. Preparing a 50-slide deck and running through them one hour before the presentation is not a plan for a meeting. It's a recipe for a dull, lifeless event that does not achieve the outcomes you hope.

CLIENT COMMUNICATIONS AND BRAND BUILDING

Diane Hessan, president and CEO of Communispace, who was introduced in Chapter 3, heads one of the fastest-growing social networking companies in the country. As you might expect, she is socially media savvy; when we sat down to talk, she had 10,000 Twitter followers. Yet Hessan doesn't rely on electronic communication to build the brand. She hits the road. Communispace is in the business of helping its clients get closer to their customers, so she's a believer in spending time with her own. "Client dedication is the number-one value," she says.

Her focus on client interaction goes back to the early days of the company, when it was still struggling to find the right business model. "It was Tom Brailsford at Hallmark," she recalls, "who came up with the idea that finally worked." Communispace was focusing on how to create virtual employee communities for companies. The client suggested that was just a "nice to have." What Hallmark *needed* was customer communities that would drive new product development.

That fortuitous comment led Hessan to become "obsessive" about seeing her clients, making it part of her brand. "Without Tom Brailsford at Hallmark, I wouldn't be here. There is no client I won't talk to on the phone. I will always meet with clients, the answer is always yes." If Communispace loses clients, Hessan picks up the phone and thanks them for the business they have sent her through the years. Her actions are a blueprint for other employees in building the brand. "I model what I want people to do," she says. "That makes the brand and culture tangible. People know what is important."

PUBLIC SPEAKING TO COMMUNICATE YOUR BRAND

Hessan is frequently invited to speak on panels and give keynote addresses. Like other successful business owners, she has a soft spot for other entrepreneurs, and she's open about the ups and downs of business. This candor endears her to people and cements her brand. "I want to give back to entrepreneurs and small businesspeople," she says, "because people were unbelievably generous with their time when I had challenges growing my business."

Public speaking is one of the most powerful ways to build your brand. It serves several strategic purposes, from business development to recruiting. "Most of the speaking I do is local, because our headquarters are here and we can recruit here," says Hessan. Speaking definitely puts Communispace on the map and attracts talent. For a 10-year-old company that is a big win. Remarks Hessan: "I do hope that by speaking, I get people to start saying, 'Communispace! I know about that company!'"

"I do hope that by speaking, I get people to start saying, 'Communispace! I know about that company!'"

BECOMING A CONFIDENT SPEAKER

How do you become a more powerful, confident speaker? Katherin Nukk-Freeman, who was introduced in Chapter 4, loves speaking today, but it wasn't always that way. Born in Chicago, Nukk-Freeman describes herself as a shy kid. Her father was a chemical engineer, and because her family moved all over the country, she loved to read and write but didn't speak up much in class. As she relates: "Teachers would tell my parents that 'we know she has the answer, but she doesn't raise her hand.'"

One day Nukk-Freeman got up and decided that shyness would no longer define her. She ran for student government and made herself practice her speeches. She won the election. Every year after that, she challenged herself to do more and more public speaking. By the time she was a senior she was completely comfortable on a stage. "It had a snowball effect," she remembers. Today, she is out speaking all the time, and she considers it one of the best ways to build her brand.

Learning to speak well is like any other skill, from golf to playing the piano. You need great coaches, the right tools, and hundreds, actually thousands, of hours to develop mastery. If you haven't yet started developing this skill, it is never too late. Seize the moment. Take a course, hire a coach, and work at it. Be sure to record and watch videotapes of your presentations so you can see where you need to improve. Experience is the best way to build confidence. The more you speak, the more confident you become.

SPEAKING AND THOUGHT LEADERSHIP

George Colony, CEO of Forrester Research, is an enthusiastic speaker. Since Forrester's brand is forward-thinking research, speaking is an effective way to drive brand recognition. How does he connect with his audiences? He's provocative. A speech to CIOs might be titled "Five Things I Would Tell Your CEO over Coffee." "He starts with a story, makes a provocative point, and conveys a message that is utterly accessible," says his vice president of communication, Karyl Levinson.

As you consider how to become a thought leader, this is a great model. Stand out by taking a position. Make people think. Engage them. It's more fun for you and for them, and it definitely builds your brand as a thought leader. Be interesting. Provide a different viewpoint. Give the talk no one else could give.

"Almost everything we say is unique to Forrester. That uniqueness is how George represents us to audiences at the executive level," says

Levinson. Colony takes personal responsibility for it. "He has pretty strong pride of authorship," Levinson explains. He researches and talks to analysts and his communications team, but in the end, it is him.

PROVIDE VALUE WHEN YOU SPEAK

"When I speak," says Lisa Matthews, of Winslow, Evans & Crocker, "it's rarely on managing your money." While she's a respected financial advisor and runs a family office for individuals and business owners, people see her as more than that. She likes to talk about topics that help people without seeming to just be selling something. There are plenty of presentations on how to invest. "I talk about how to manage transition, or how to build a business," she says.

> "Almost everything we say is unique to Forrester. That uniqueness is how George represents us to audiences at the executive level," says Levinson. "He has pretty strong pride of authorship," Levinson explains. He researches, talks to analysts, and his communications team, but in the end, it is him."

Offer up your expertise in a way that really helps others. Talking about high-interest topics will win you more speaking opportunities with the right audiences. You'll earn a reputation as a good speaker, which will prompt more invitations. That supports brand building. You can't be everywhere, so choose venues where you can make an impact. You can always find time for public speaking if it fits in with your overall brand-building strategy.

MEDIA INTERVIEWS

Media is the way to reach broad audiences. Many corporate leaders are afraid of media, but they shouldn't be. If you know what you're doing, interviews are an excellent way to raise your profile and build your brand.

The media are interested in issues and trends. Instead of waiting for the call from them, why not have your team pitch high-interest topics?

Position yourself as an expert. By doing that, you control the conversation. Be the one out in front. That is part of your role as CEO or leader of your organization. Taking positions in the media definitely builds your brand.

Bob Kelly, CEO of BNY Mellon, was invited in 2009 to come to the White House with other financial executives. It was in the midst of the fallout from the financial crisis. At that meeting, he reached out to Richard K. Davis, CEO of U.S. Bancorp. "Davis is a high-integrity person; his company was healthy, too," remarks Kelly. "I said, 'Right now, the spokespersons for our industry are the companies that are in trouble.'" The two men agreed it would be appropriate and helpful for them to take the microphone. After their meeting with the president, they stood on the lawn of the White House and spoke with national reporters for two hours.

Some might shirk from such a role, but Kelly did it because it was the right thing for this industry. "It is intellectually challenging. You don't know what is coming at you," he says. Kelly sees it as good for his company and also good for the industry.

PUBLIC COMPANY CEOS

As a leader in a public company, you do have constraints. If you are new in a leadership role, it is important to get media training and to have ongoing media support from a public relations specialist. Make sure you are always on message and know how to manage a high-stakes interview.

When Constant Contact went public in October 2007, Gail Goodman had to retrain for a new and higher-stakes arena. She had a candid, down-to-earth style, but she didn't want to say anything that would hurt the stock price, or inadvertently send the wrong message.

"I didn't change my style, but I did have to be dramatically more cognizant of how we communicated externally," she says. "I also had to learn to work with an entirely different audience: Wall Street. I had a lot of good help and coaching from others."

Erika Dornaus, Goodman's public relations lead, says Goodman is adept at soliciting advice and analyzing whether interviews or speaking engagements are important to her and to the brand.

Learn to handle the media and you'll find it can be one of the most powerful brand-building opportunities you have. Also, get crisis training. Any leader in a public or private company who might be speaking to the media in a crisis should be trained once every year or two. A crisis doesn't have to bring down your company, and a well-handled event can even improve your company's brand and reputation.

TIPS ON MEDIA INTERVIEWS

- Make sure the media topic connects to your brand strategy.
- When you can, choose outlets where you can speak courageously and be quoted accurately.
- Prepare well and know the talking points.
- Be clear and succinct in presenting your opinion.
- If you aren't comfortable, get busy learning how to be.
- Hire a coach and get training.
- Surround yourself with a good team who can help you.
- Say yes to low-risk interviews, and build your confidence.
- Anticipate the questions you will be asked.
- Always bridge back to key messages.

I'm not suggesting that you jump out in front every time an industry issue arises. But as a former television reporter, I watched the way leaders who spoke to the media on controversial subjects earned respect. Building a higher profile and speaking up on important issues not only enhances your brand in the media, your willingness to do so can be seen as a positive distinction among your employees, clients, analysts, regulators, and the public.

Many leaders don't realize the positive boomerang effect that good media has on employees. Employees take pride in working for a company where the CEO and other leaders are respected for standing up and speaking about issues. They want to work for a company whose executives are regarded as thought leaders, because he or she has opinions on important industry trends. That says, "You're working for a winner." As a leader, your thought leadership reflects well on them.

CEO NETWORKING

Many leaders are aware of the fact that it is important to network inside and outside of their companies, but they often don't take the time to create the connections that could serve them well in their roles, and at the same time, build brand recognition. Don't look at networking as just going to dinners or parties and shaking hands. Think of it as connecting with people every day, in a variety of ways. CEO networking is really about creating genuine relationships that are mutually beneficial. CEOs with strong brands have powerful networks.

It pays to look at networking as something you do all the time—as part of who you are. This is what my client Steve Baker does. One of his favorite quotes is: "You can't cross the sea merely by standing and staring at the water." Baker is never standing and staring. He is an innovative architect with a quest for adventure and a real interest in other people. As a result, he's built a list of clients across the globe from Europe to Asia to the Middle East.

One of my favorite stories is how he networked to open the doors to "the Kingdom." As an American architect with no Middle East ties, he managed to be selected by the Saudi royal family to design a major public building. He was flying to a furniture manufacturing conference in Detroit. On the plane, a woman in a veil gave him a long, focused look. He nodded and the woman nodded back.

"Walking out of the airport, one of my team members came up to say he'd been sitting next to that same woman and had an incredible conversation with her." Baker followed up immediately, and the woman asked him to send a digital copy of Baker Design Group's architectural portfolio. The next thing he knew, the Saudi royal family was asking Baker to put in a proposal for a 2.5-million-square-foot hospital complex.

Baker called a friend from Egypt to get tips on how to conduct himself in a meeting in a culture so foreign to him. He was planning to pay for his own trip. The friend was effusive. "You don't know what that means to them. To offer to fly your team there to hear about their challenges and ambitions . . . will be taken in the most honorable way."

Baker's team arrived during the holy week of Ramadan. They were welcomed like old friends. The woman in the veil greeted him warmly.

She led the discussion. Their proposal won. Baker believes that going out of his way to show respect and getting in the door with an idea that wowed them were the reasons they won, over some formidable competitors.

One quality that Baker exudes—part of his brand—is a genuine interest in others. As a child, he actually had a severe stuttering problem, one that lingered into adulthood. "The speech impediment was the obstacle to being accepted," he says. However, stuttering also sensitized him to what others were feeling or thinking. And that became an asset as he built relationships.

Baker eschews the classic networking activities like golfing, dinner, and parties, but he strives to make "real" connections with people in everyday situations. He notes that "when you approach people as special individuals with ambitions that you can help make come true, you're successful." Understanding what other people want and giving it to them has built Steve Baker's business. "It isn't just a personal trait, it's a brand differentiator," he says.

> Understanding what other people want and giving it to them has built Steve Baker's business. "It isn't just a personal trait, it's a brand differentiator," he says.

NETWORKS ARE BRAND ASSETS

Your network is a tremendous asset, and you should treat it like gold. Make genuine connections with other industry leaders, policy makers, clients, government officials, and others. Don't look at the effort as drudgery. Look at it as making friends and really get to know people.

That's exactly what Lisa Matthews did to build her successful financial advisory business. In fact, she's asked so often how she built such a strong network that she now delivers a presentation called "Building Your Business by Building a Community." Here's an example of how she met someone and helped him get what he wanted, leveraging one connection into many.

"I had lunch with Paul Guzzi, the new president of the Boston Chamber of Commerce. He took three hours and gave me the lay of the land." At the end of the meeting he told Matthews he needed her help in getting a new Women's Advisory Council at the Chamber of Commerce up and running, and she agreed. In return, Matthews asked Guzzi to introduce her to three people at every meeting.

Matthews also built her network by serving on boards such as the Walker School for Children and the Home for Little Wanderers. She looked at organizations that she was genuinely interested in. She facilitates the Boston chapter of Women Presidents Organization (WPO) because "I have a passion for helping women entrepreneurs." The connections support her business model. "I'm a connector—I connect people," she remarks.

Being truly interested in other people is what makes you successful at networking. It is also important to pursue your passions, and connect with other people who care about the same things. I remember seeing Diane Hessan, the CEO of Communispace, speaking at an event her organization was sponsoring for Horizons for Homeless Children. I was so impressed by her passion. It was obvious that the commitment was a personal one. This was very clear to her audience, as well. She was genuinely connected to the cause. When people see your passion it makes a strong brand impression. They are more inclined to want to connect with you and do business with you because they know what you stand for.

BUILDING BRAND "AWARENESS"

All of the communication strategies we've examined in this chapter help you build brand awareness. Brand awareness is a marketing concept that measures other people's knowledge of a brand's existence.

BUILD A NETWORK THAT HELPS YOU BUILD YOUR LEADERSHIP BRAND

What Issues are Important to you?

_____

_____

_____

How does this connect with your brand?

_____

_____

_____

Name three boards or organizations that would align with your interests and your brand:

1. _____

_____

_____

2. _____

_____

_____

3. _____

_____

_____

Your leadership brand is most valuable when it is known by many others. That's why communication skills are so essential. As a leader you need to be able to communicate well in a variety of forums, with all kinds of people. Over time, as you put yourself in situations where you need to learn new skills, you become more confident and self-assured. The reward is that people get to know you, your name springs to mind, and your brand becomes strong, when people think of leaders in your industry.

Make the decision to gain the skills and experience you need to command every situation. Don't avoid the spotlight, embrace it. Carve out time, and make communication priority one.

In the next chapter, we'll look at the less traditional and fast-growing world of social media and how you can leverage it to build your brand.

CHAPTER SUMMARY

- You can change the culture if you communicate brand values.
- Public speaking is a great way to build a brand.
- The best way to build a brand is to show thought leadership.
- Provide your audiences with value, and be provocative.
- Take advantage of the media to raise your profile.
- Networking is an effective way to communicate your brand.

Social Media and Brand—What Today's CEO Must Know

By giving people the power to share, we're making the

world more transparent.

—MARK ZUCKERBERG

THE TV SERIES MAD MEN, SET IN NEW YORK CITY in the 1960s, is a sexy, stylized, and provocative drama about a bygone era when ruthlessly competitive men and women of Madison Avenue competed with catchy slogans, snazzy posters, and giant billboards. That was branding then. My, how things have changed! Building a commercial brand today is about a lot more than taglines, printed brochures, and magazine ads.

The "social world" has revolutionized branding. Digital communication has broken down barriers, making it easier and faster than ever to reach millions of people. The world is sharing information. Mark Zuckerberg's vision is real. And in terms of branding, you can look like a giant sitting home and running a business from a single computer. That's why a CEO in the information age has to understand how and when to participate in new media. The movement toward transparency and a demand for authenticity in the "social" world has a profound impact on your brand.

There's a lot of confusion, misinformation, and anxiety about the social world. Many leaders are wondering what to do, what not to bother doing, and where to start. Whether or not you're ready, you have to embrace it. There is a conversation going on in cyberspace. People are talking about you and your company. It is happening in real time, 24/7. You can choose not to participate, but the conversation will go on without you, and that can do real harm to your brand.

A few CEOs and leaders are jumping into the "social" world. As I write today, this is still rare. Most are still waiting, wondering, and thinking. Some are wishing it would go away. Meanwhile, Twitter, YouTube, Facebook, blogging, and LinkedIn are taking over the online world. People are spending enormous amounts of time online. Look at it this way: to build a brand, go where the people are. When it comes to social media, you may as well get in the game.

At the company level, most organizations are mapping out and executing strategies for social networking, marketing, and media. Your plans should include building the brand of the company and also the brands of *individual leaders*. The paragraphs that follow describe how to participate and move forward building your individual leader brand.

IS THERE A FORMULA FOR SUCCESS IN SOCIAL MEDIA, MARKETING, AND NETWORKING?

The Internet and the burgeoning number of social media and social networking opportunities have transformed corporate brand management. As I write today, there are 500 million active participants on Facebook, 80 million on LinkedIn, and 145 million registered users on Twitter. Those numbers will quickly be out of date. With so many people spending more and more of their time online, companies are becoming very creative in reaching their target markets. So it only stands to reason that, as a leader, you can take advantage of the same dynamic to build your brand.

"SOCIAL" CEO GUIDELINES

- Get educated about social marketing, networking, and media.
- Make sure people in the organization are on top of trends.

- Establish the goals for your company.
- Think of these as tools for creating an online community.
- Look at it as a way to widen your circle of influence.
- Be early enough to gain competitive advantage.
- Look at every technology in terms of how you can leverage it.
- Everything you do in cyberspace should reflect well on your personal and company brand.
- Don't allow fear or ignorance to keep you from gaining a competitive advantage with a tool.
- Tap your team and your network to put you in a position to be successful with the tools.
- Evaluate how they are working by setting targets and tracking performance.

It would be unwise to choose just one or two social media channels. New ones keep roaring onto the scene. For example, think of all the people who can't live without their iPads. A couple of years ago those devices didn't exist. Soon, somthing else will come along that people embrace and can't remember how they lived without it. That's why it is important to take advantage of many of the tools available today. With change happening so fast, it would be impossible to provide a perfect plan for building your brand through social marketing and media. What you should do depends on where the people are whom you want to reach. The best way to develop your strategy is to think about what your employees, customers, industry leaders and others are and follow them.

Why is it important to get out of your comfort zone? People who are 20 years old today believe e-mail is old school. They don't like to talk on the phone—they rarely check their voice mail, because their primary form of communication is texting and Facebook. Remember IM? Instant messaging? That was Generation Y. It's come and gone. So you need to be current, and watch how communication preferences evolve.

Your plan will be constantly changing, and always based on the strategy of reaching the people you want to reach. If you always keep your target audience in mind, making informed choices will be easier. To accomplish this, you don't need to become an expert, but you do need to have people on your team who are current. Don't base your decisions purely on your own preferences. Listen to what the experts have to say. They'll support your effort to build your brand.

HOW MANY CEOs ARE "SOCIAL"?

According to UberCEO, a website that follows, comments, and reports on CEOs who influence the business world, the number of CEOs who are "social" was very low as recently as 2009. UberCEO looked at *Fortune's* 2009 list of the top 100 CEOs to determine how many were using Facebook, Twitter, LinkedIn, Wikipedia, or had a blog, there was at that time a "miserable level of engagement."

- Only two CEOs had Twitter accounts.
- Thirteen had LinkedIn profiles, and of those, only three had more than 10 connections.
- Eighty-one percent of CEOs didn't have a personal Facebook page.
- Three-quarters of the CEOs had some kind of Wikipedia entry, but nearly a third of those had limited or outdated information.
- Not one Fortune 100 CEO had a blog.

Most big-company CEOs still didn't have what you would call a social profile. You couldn't look them up in the usual social media places like LinkedIn. Six top CEOs had let their Twitter accounts go defunct, and none had any obvious presence on Facebook or LinkedIn. Even Eric Schmidt of Google was an infrequent Twitterer and not a blogger. Steve Ballmer at Microsoft had no blog and no Twitter account. Steve Jobs of Apple and Larry Ellison of Oracle had no Twitter, Facebook, LinkedIn, or blog presences, according to Forrester Research.

WHY CEOs AREN'T GOING SOCIAL YET

The reluctance to go "social" in public companies is obviously driven by concerns about guidance, misguidance, or releasing sensitive information. There's a general feeling that going social simply isn't necessary and could be harmful. In the age of the Sarbanes-Oxley Act and Reg-FD (Fair Disclosure), public company CEOs wouldn't find any compelling reason to engage in anything that they perceive could inadvertently put their companies at risk.

On blogging, time is also a consideration. It takes time to understand what blogging is all about; develop a strategy for it; generate topics that are safe and interesting; and then, there's the challenge of writing regularly. CEOs of all companies, no matter what the size, are busy people.

If you aren't using social media, the entire purpose of it may elude you, especially when considering what is the best use of your time. Many people over age 35 regard it as absurd to take time to "tweet" about their whereabouts (which by the way is not the best use of Twitter). As far as social networking on sites such as LinkedIn, CEOs and top leaders guard their "friend" networks. They work hard to build key relationships, and they aren't inclined to open up their database to the "outside world when they get requests for introductions from strangers.

At the same time, there is a legitimate reason to think that eventually CEOs will start using social media and networking. It will happen if leaders begin to see social media as a strategic tool in communicating and building their brands. If they begin to see other companies achieving business objectives, there will be a movement to embrace it. Social media will also become more and more prevalent as a reputation management tool. CEOs have had a tough time in the media battling negative press about salaries, bonuses, and business practices. A blog, well done, along with other appropriate social media, could be a potent tool in countering negative PR.

As I researched the current thinking about CEOs and social media, I read a number of articles that posited that CEOs were "afraid of" or "ignorant" about social media. I don't think that accurately describes the objection. After working closely with leaders for more than 10 years, I know that CEOs are cautious when there is so much at stake. They may not be early adopters, but most CEOs I know are curious people, interested in new ideas and technology. Many today are experimenting with internal blogs and video newsletters; that is a good stepping stone to learning about new potent tools of communication.

The conversation is going on all around you. Other companies are looking at what to do and when. If you are a public company, you already know that your customers, fans, and detractors are talking about you, and you probably have some measures in place to stay on top of it and respond to it. In the context of your own personal brand management, you also want to be in on the conversation and able to participate when appropriate. One question to ask yourself is, "What will people find when they go looking for me online?" Are there feature articles? Bylines? Op-eds? Videos? Speeches on YouTube? These days, people make decisions about your brand based on your visibility in social media. That's why you need someone in your company to be in charge of managing your social public profile. Ideally, there are many places where people can get accurate information and an impression about you, not only on your website, but in other places they search.

TO BLOG, OR NOT TO BLOG?

With apologies to Shakespeare, that is the question most leaders are asking me right now. A blog, short for "Web log," is often described as a diary online. But that doesn't adequately summarize what it is, or more importantly, what a blog can do for your leadership brand. You can make it a great tool, if you know how to use it. And I don't mean writing about what you had for breakfast or the adventures of your dog.

The way to approach writing a blog is to identify topics that are aligned with, and build your personal brand. If you don't enjoy writing, then blogging may at first seem like a chore. It is possible to collaborate with a good writer on your team and still make it personal, in your voice. And, if you do like to write, a blog is a perfect vehicle for communicating brand values. You can publish whenever you like, talk about topics you want to cover, without the constraint of waiting for traditional media to call you. Your personal blog is one tool that can help you to initiate, and in many ways manage the conversation about your company. It also keeps your brand and your company's brand fresh and relevant in the minds of readers, who are your employees, clients, and customers, other CEOs, industry leaders, and the media.

The brilliance of blogs isn't just the ability to publish but also the ability to see who is and how many people are reading and responding to what you say. You can gauge their response to your message by their comments. A good blog gets a following, which enables you to build communities of people who are interested in you and your company. And on Twitter, which is really microblogging, you can also generate discussions, see how people respond, and track followers by name.

One important note: people expect *you* to write the blog. If you have other people collaborating with you on the blog, be mindful of the fact that it still needs to represent your ideas and sound like you. Your tone and cadence need to be there. Spend time with the person who is writing it to be sure he or she is capturing your message your way. They have the responsibility of representing you to the world. In Chapter 11, I talk more about this and offer advice on how to work with a writer.

In the virtual world, people expect authenticity. It's also a mistake to give sales pitches in a blog. People don't like that. They are attuned to "phoniness" and reject anything that seems too promotional. The topics you choose should be interesting, timely, on trend, personal, and filled with insights. Readers will visit a few times and make up their minds quickly about whether it is worth their time.

A lot has been made of the fact that younger generations demand transparency. In my experience, this is now a universal expectation. People of all ages have an expectation that CEOs and leaders should be more forthcoming in their communication and more accessible to people at all levels. In addition, most people have a sixth sense about the authenticity of your writing. If it sounds like it was penned by your PR team, it simply won't gain as much traction. I'm not suggesting that you have to do all the writing, but if you do decide to go in this direction, better to make it real, than too perfect.

WHAT'S AHEAD IN THE SOCIAL MEDIA WORLD?

Who knows? Naturally, some social media, marketing, and networking channels will go the way of the eight-track tape (or soon the CD). And, there's no question that the Internet is still the Wild Wild West—an uncharted frontier where a Harvard student can launch a "social network" and within six years be sitting on a private company with 500 million active users valued at $50 billion by some estimates (Facebook's Mark Zuckerberg). What's next? How can we possibly know? We only know it will keep coming.

Regardless of the "fad" nature of some social media and marketing, there are questions you can start to think about now. For example, if you're going to write a blog, start reading the newspaper; think about how you would comment on current events in your industry. When you travel, jot down notes about things you'd like to write about, whether it's an internal blog for your employees or an external blog that anyone can read.

DEFINITIONS

It's important to understand the distinctions among the terms social networking, social marketing, and social media. Get familiar with the information below before developing your social strategy.

Social Networking

A social network focuses on building relationships through the Internet among people who often share common interests or activities. Internet networking happens on Facebook, LinkedIn, Twitter, Google Groups, and any other place where people want to gather and have a conversation or connect with other people.

The process of building online communities through groups and friends lists can also take place on websites and blogs that set out to create virtual communities. It's a way of sharing information between two or more individuals in any online community.

Social Marketing

The best way to define *social marketing* is to think of it as marketing and advertising that reaches potential consumers via websites they visit for other purposes. That includes advertising on social networking websites such as

Facebook. The ads can be targeted based on keywords in users' profiles to match their stated interests or recent activities.

Social marketers are getting savvier, and so is the sophistication of the software they use to reach customers. Today, if you go shopping, whether it's for Jimmy Choo shoes or a Harley-Davidson motorcycle, you're likely to see an ad pop up on one of your favorite media websites, in the spot reserved for targeted advertising. To the average person that looks like magic. We can only imagine what else is on the horizon as the Internet becomes a dominant advertising realm.

Social Media

Social media is essentially any information published or posted, which is widely available to the public. This includes self-published work, as well as writing and reporting by others, vetted or simply offered through traditional or social media. Any words, pictures, audio, or video that people outside your company can access is social media.

There are more and more software tools that allow you to disseminate information, from wikis to blogs to podcasts. YouTube is social media. Blogs are social media. These are, in Web parlance, "user-generated content." There are a million definitions, and today social media includes the traditional media outlets that now publish online. What glues it all together? It's in the public domain. If you have a computer, an iPad, a netbook, a BlackBerry, or a Kindle, you can usually retrieve it.

As you move forward, and social media tools change, one thing will never be altered: your brand. Think about what you write. How will it build your brand? How will it be viewed by the people you want to influence? Wherever social media goes, you need a social strategy.

YOUR SOCIAL STRATEGY

Your social strategy will evolve as technology changes and new tools are introduced Still it makes no sense to wait until everything is in place, if you want a social presence now. The best way to start, is just to start.

Create a social presence and begin to attract and nurture a community of followers interested in you and your company. The sooner you start, the sooner you will reach the people who buy your products and services, want to work for you, or do business with you.

Your strategy should always begin with your purpose and your target audience. Once you know what you want to accomplish, figure out where to find the people you want to reach. Then, put together a plan and a team to help you do that. Perhaps a light touch of "social" will be more than enough in the beginning. You'll gain some know-how. You will have a presence, and that may be more than your competitors are doing. The first forays will give you the experience to leverage what you know into new areas. The more you do, the more you'll understand how to capitalize on the branding opportunities that social provides.

Gaining experience will provide you with "raw" feedback about your company, information that you can use right now. Social media and marketing can provide you with fast, real-time feedback that is difficult to obtain through traditional marketing and research projects such as focus groups and surveys. Timely feedback keeps you from becoming insulated and allows you to react quickly to perceptions or feedback, whether it's coming from employees, customers, or the public. Getting information in a timely way is a huge competitive advantage. Starting and participating in social conversations creates an impression that you care and are connected. You can, if appropriate, respond in a personal way to defuse issues and avoid allowing misinformation to flourish. You can also speak from the heart about issues that matter to you. The timeliness of social media also allows you to get out front and establish thought leadership on issues. And even if you are only using electronic communication to reach internal audiences, an employee blog can give you a powerful forum for talking about what's happening in the business, focusing people's attention on key drivers of success, and highlighting values and behaviors essential to your company. There are a myriad of ways you can make social media work for you.

If you are a leader in a smaller company, you probably don't feel the constraints that public company leaders do. You're ready to jump in with both feet. You may even feel frustrated because you wish you already had a huge blog and Twitter following. The most important step you can take is to get help to do what you want to do, if you don't have the expertise on your team. Don't hand off your corporate reputation to a public relations firm but work with trusted partners on an outsource basis to help you create your strategy and take advantage of all that social media and marketing can do for you.

Anyone can find the time and resources to leverage social media and build a brand, if the goals are clear and you have the right people to help. There is no single path to "social" success, but I hope these insights and ideas will guide your thinking. Craft an approach to the online presence that will make you proud.

BASELINE ASSESSMENT

The quickest way to assess your brand online is to do a Web search for your name, and also go to YouTube, which is second only to Google as a search engine of choice. You'll quickly learn whether you're on the radar and, if you are, what is being said. You'll see what articles are written, blog comments posted, and videos available. Most people only research the first two or three pages of Google and the first page or two of YouTube, so in five to ten minutes you'll have a baseline.

You want to know this because this is what potential employees, customers, vendors, analysts, investors, and the media see when they go looking for you and your company, what you see is what they see. They're checking out your personal profile, reading what is said about you, and watching your videos. Do you like what they are reading and seeing? If not, what can you do about that? If you don't have a presence at all, that sends a message about whether you and your company are in the stream of the online world. As we move rapidly forward to a time when most information is online, staying out of the social world will be more difficult and more risky. Eventually a leader's absence from social media will be seen as curious, perhaps aloof, not as accessible or transparent as some of his or her counterparts.

HOW CEOs ARE USING BLOGS NOW

The CEOs that are blogging are using this medium in different ways. The following are some examples.

- Craig Newmark, the "Craig" behind Craigslist, has made his blog a forum to promote causes he cares about, from veterans of Afghanistan to fighting AIDS in Kenya. His father died of lung cancer, so he promoted a *Bold and the Beautiful* episode on CBS on the topic. He talks about Open Government, an idea that promotes full disclosure of what's going on in government and where the money goes. These things are personally important to him, and so he's made advocacy part of his leadership brand.
- On Blogmaverick.com, Mark Cuban, owner of the Dallas Mavericks, posts once a week, often sports rants about what's wrong with college football. But he tackles more esoteric business topics, such as what's wrong with monetary policy at the Federal Reserve. And he's not afraid of weighing in on why Bristol Palin could win on *Dancing with the Stars* (although she ultimately did not).
- Mark Zuckerberg, founder of Facebook, used his blog to apologize for releasing a feature called Beacon, Facebook's then-controversial ad-targeting system, which he said was a mistake to launch at that time. He used the forum to tell critics he heard them and to explain what Facebook had done to improve it.
- Ross Mayfield, chairman and founder of Socialtext, has a high-quality blog called *Markets, Technology & Musings* at Ross .typepad.com that offers insights on industry trends. It's a nice way to establish thought leadership. Then again, you would hope the guy who started the first wiki company would be savvy about this.
- Tony Hsieh, CEO of Zappos and author of a bestselling book, is often mentioned on the topic of leader blog lists. Zappos is the company that made shoe buying on the Internet easy. After Amazon.com acquired Zappos, Hseih kept blogging for Zappos in 2010, mainly about goings-on at the company. The blog posts were well-written pieces that gave outsiders the feeling they were peeking in on the inside.

- Michael Dell reportedly uses his blog to start two-way conversations that have made Dell a powerhouse in the PC industry. That's worth noting, because he has leveraged blogs as a customer relationship tool. Blogs are not a one-way street. You get feedback, and you can use it to gather incredibly valuable information about how people see your company.

GEORGE COLONY, FORRESTER, A GREAT BLOGGER

George Colony, whom you met in previous chapters, makes good use of social media, maintaining an outstanding, relevant, personal blog and a presence on Twitter, which really is a microblog. He's a thought leader in the blogosphere. As a matter of fact, Colony writes an insightful series about the "The Social CEO," in which he shares his opinion about CEO blogging.

"I think the CEO should be social," he says. "You should have a social profile because you're in the business now of hiring Generations X and Y, people ages 18 to 28, they live and breathe social." No doubt, social media and networking are the oxygen that the next generations breathe, so before they do anything, including going on an interview at a new company, the first thing they do is look for the CEO's social profile, including Twitter posts and blogs.

"It's important in the coming age of high transparency that the leader be able to state the values of the company beyond the letter in the annual report," advises Colony. "You just have to make sure that what you say in social media is congruent with your brand and your company brand." Colony also believes social media savviness has nothing to do with age. "If you look at Bill Marriott's blog, he's 70, and you can tell [the blog] comes from his voice."

The ability to be provocative makes Colony a successful blogger. It's about authenticity. He's candid and opinionated. "Right now, I'm talking about how the Web is a dying technology, soon to be replaced by the app Internet. That tells me that Google is in trouble, Amazon is in trouble. Having courage means you have to do the research, and understand, you can't take potshots, but you have to tell it like it is," says Colony.

Colony is thrilled when the blog makes an impact. "Back in 1998, I was quoted as saying Amazon was toast, because Barnes & Noble would attack them. Jeff Bezos [of Amazon] wrote in one of his books that [that] was an incredibly pivotal moment. It inspired him. He realized he needed to redouble his effort." Now, that's impact!

If you're going to write a blog, you want to be sure people read it. Being controversial is one way to make sure you get a following. Even if you choose to be more informative than controversial, make sure your stamp is all over it. While you certainly can have help developing ideas and with writing and editing, the essence of the blog's content has to come from you.

IS NOW THE RIGHT TIME?

Feedback from blogs and Twitter can be more potent than marketing studies that cost you a fortune. It can give you direct access to your customers and why they are or are not happy. So, now is the right time if you want to get some valuable market research and you've determined that blogging is a fit with your brand. Perhaps you'd like to use your blog as a research tool. Perhaps you want to establish thought leadership. Perhaps you have a book you want to promote to build your brand. Maybe blogging is a way to make a more direct connection with your customers.

Make an informed decision. Bring together a team of knowledgeable people to talk about your social strategy. Think about who you want to reach, what you want to dedicate in terms of time and resources, and get started. Once the system is set up, you shouldn't have to spend more than a few minutes a day, if you have the right support.

HOW TO START WRITING

One strategy you can employ is my technique of "writing out loud." This works in speechwriting, media interviews, really any form of communication that has to come from you. When executive coaches from Bates Communications get together with our clients, we'll turn on the tape recorder, ask questions, and record the exact words our clients say. This ensures that we are capturing the authentic ideas, words, and cadence of the leader.

You can also make your own writing more authentic and efficient if you record your words, your way. You don't need a coach, but it is helpful to have an interviewer. A CEO I know works with his executive communications team. Several times he has been able to sit down with them, turn on a tape recorder, and answer their questions. They transcribe and edit what he says and work it into his blog and speeches. As to how often to write, the more you do it the better you get. And if you are writing for a blog remember you need to be a regular or you won't gain a following. Be realistic about your busy schedule, but consider writing once a week, or twice a month, to begin. Set up a system for capturing your ideas with someone on your team handling the editing and posting. Leverage everything you write—for example, consider making your blog posts into articles, tweets, and even videos.

MANAGING "SOCIAL" RISK

How can you take advantage of social media and not also avoid unnecessary risk that puts your brand reputation at stake? The following is by no means an exhaustive list, just a few things to think about and address.

- The first risk is to represent the brand and not overwhelm the brand or become "the story." If you stay focused on providing real insights and are thoughtful about what's best for your company, this shouldn't be a concern. You can be provocative and still represent your brand well.
- Another risk is to get too far out in front of your company, your industry, or your constituents. What you say has to be aligned with your company's values, brand, and strategic plan. Don't create confusion in the minds of your readers about where you stand on the value and strength of your company.
- There are many complex issues facing your company and industry that are not appropriate for a blog. Be courageous and candid in providing thought leadership, without making people wonder what on earth you were thinking when you wrote that. This is where it is important to have a thoughtful group of people who

support you and can keep you from saying something that either doesn't sound real or is too far "out there."

- Some leaders are using social media to promote social causes, and that's great—if it is part of your brand. My advice would be to talk mostly about business issues and trends, because it is more relevant to your brand.

- The same thing applies for commenting on politics: avoid talking about political issues unless that is part of your brand and your strategy. That isn't to say you *never* should do so, just think twice before writing political commentary. If you sit down to write when you're angry, think before you hit the Publish button.

- If you have regulars who comment, be sure to monitor and see that they aren't cranks who are taking your words and misinterpreting or misusing them or using the blog just to promote themselves.

TWITTER POWER

Diane Hessan, who was discussed in Chapter 7, doesn't blog. She does, as previously mentioned, use Twitter, a service that allows you to post an idea in 140-character "tweets." "I use social media because it's practicing what we preach," says Hessan. "If you want to communicate online, Twitter is a great vehicle for us and for me because it is very unobtrusive. My following somebody is no sweat for them, and somebody following me is no sweat."

MORE REASONS TO BE "SOCIAL"

These days, there are plenty of reasons to go social. If you haven't found a reason yet, here are a few more.

Create Intimacy

It may seem counterintuitive to think that electronic media can help you create intimacy, but when done well, social media and networking are a superb way to create a connection with your customers, employees, vendors, and investors.

Recruit Employees

Virtual presence can create strong social bonds with people. Your presence on social media creates interest and reduces the "mystery" about you.

Appear Current

This concern is more important to some CEOs than to others. Right now there aren't many CEOs active in social media, so having a personal online presence can make you look hip.

Build Community

Web-based communication is powerful because of what it isn't as much as what it is. As mentioned, marketing used to be a one-way street. No more. It's a two-way conversation.

Hessan had about 11,000 followers at the time we met, many of them clients. Her tweets to them take about 15 minutes a day. She doesn't just talk about her company. "I'm trying to be real and talk about things going on in my life," she says. "It's not just market research, not just touting how great we are. I talk about our culture, our fun, our new research, and I also talk about going to hear my daughter's choir, and I talk about baseball and politics. I think people like that I'm talking about me, and not just using it to shill."

On Twitter, a majority of posts you see are, frankly, trivial. But you don't have to follow anyone. Or you can decide to follow just a few people you respect. You control that part. And on the other side of the coin, people who want to find you will find you. It is challenging to say anything meaningful in 140 characters (that's letters and spaces, not words). One way to manage that limitation is to send out daily quotes, post links to your latest blog post, or promote appearances.

ALLOWING YOUR PRODUCTS TO BE THE "STAR"

When you have a "cool" product, you may just decide to let it be the star of the show. iRobot was founded in 1990 when Massachusetts Institute of

Technology roboticists Colin Angle and Helen Greiner teamed up with their professor, Dr. Rodney Brooks, with the vision of making practical robots a reality.

In 2009, the company generated more than $298 million in revenue and employed more than 500 of the robot industry's top professionals, including mechanical, electrical, and software engineers and related support staff. iRobot stock trades on the Nasdaq Stock Market under the ticker symbol IRBT.

"I think the robots do a better job social networking than I do," says Angle. "Roomba has a Facebook page and 2,000 videos posted about its ability to transport animals." Social marketing is a huge part of the iRobot brand. The robot takes center stage. "It is a good virtual brand," observes Angle, "because people are passionate about robots, and if you're passionate about robots, you know about iRobot."

iRobot's social media presence generates interest from the traditional media and vice versa. Their robots have been spoofed by *Saturday Night Live,* have appeared on *The Daily Show* several times, and have made movie appearances, too. However, it would be a mistake to attribute this brand power to luck. What's behind it is the CEO and his vision to create a fun company that builds cool things.

The cool factor also is a deciding factor in how Angle communicates through social media and with live audiences. He gives talks with live demonstrations. They get captured for the company's website or posted on YouTube. "Probably my primary method of communicating is through interactive speeches and presentations," says Angle, "because I really enjoy people asking questions. I enjoy telling stories about how the company developed, and it works well for me."

Angle says e-mails and blogs don't work as well for him. If you have a robot, use it! He prefers to put energy into broadcasting an all-hands presentation and making it highly interactive. Angle thinks that "that's authentic, it feels right, and it comes across believable and real and has some texture to it."

iRobot's strategy will always be to build cool things that demand attention, then, let the social media's virtual world do its thing. "That gives us an authenticity that we enjoy," says Angle.

KEEPING A LOW PROFILE

Many CEOs have explicit policies and a long-standing practice of keeping a low profile in the media. When I was sending out queries for interviews for this book, I frequently ran into this policy. It is dictated not so much by industry but by corporate culture and the individual preference of the leader. Sometimes it's just a practice that's been part of the company for generations of leaders. Other times, CEOs choose a low profile because of perceived threats, privacy, competitive issues, or the classified work they do. These are all strategic decisions.

With social media, however, you may find that even as a low-profile executive, there is a fit, because of the degree of control you have in publishing your own message. You can't control how people respond, but you can monitor what they say and take swift action if there is controversy or reason for concern. All these factors highlight the need to have a strong media relations department, team, or person on your staff. They should be well versed in both traditional media and social media.

As risky as a social presence can be, the risk of being absent can be higher. Many media relations battles will be fought going forward in the social media world. Good media relations allow you to get out in front of a crisis and manage the message. You may choose to say little, but if you get ahead of the story you have a far better chance of controlling the message.

You are the face and voice of the company. You are also the keeper of your own brand. You have to decide the best course for you. As a leader in the information age, you have the power to participate in the conversation and help define your brand and help build your company's reputation. The time to think about what you want to do is now. Consider how social media can help you to build a powerful brand and leverage that to the benefit of your organization.

In the next chapter, we'll look at how you can avoid creating a brand disaster.

CHAPTER SUMMARY

- People are plugged in, and they are having conversations about you whether you are a global company or a fast-growing national company.
- Lacking information, people make assumptions about you.
- Social marketing, networking, and media are a great way to build a brand.
- What you say and what you do are out there.
- People are influenced by what they see and read when they look you up on a Web search.
- Social media is a participatory, democratic process.
- People expect transparency and authenticity. They don't want to be manipulated.
- The way to build a great brand is to be accessible, authentic, and real.

CEO Brand "Disaster Avoidance Kit"—Do No Harm

It takes 20 years to build a reputation and five minutes to ruin it. If you think about that, you'll do things differently.

—WARREN BUFFETT

WHAT DO TIGER WOODS, MARTHA STEWART, AND TONY HAYWARD all have in common? Their brands were marred (sometimes temporarily, sometimes permanently) by brand disasters—missteps that mushroomed into reputational nightmares. In some cases (the iconic Martha comes to mind), they have made a comeback, even enhancing their reputations. Others never see redemption.

While we all love a comeback story, surviving a reputational crisis isn't the easiest way to build a brand. How do you avoid it? The golden rule is: first, do no harm to your reputation, and treat your brand like gold; then, understand how to react when there is a crisis. Whether the damage is a self-inflicted wound or an unexpected event, you need to know how to react. In this chapter we'll look at famous brand disasters—some that turned out well, and others that didn't—to see what we can learn from them.

Becoming the leader of any organization is a lot like getting married to a company. Your reputation and the reputation of the enterprise are tied together as one. Just like a marriage, the relationship is for better or worse. You're all tangled up; it's complicated. And sometimes, unfortunately, it ends in divorce.

If the public crisis is self-inflicted, you will get less sympathy, but people are still willing to forgive, and often do with a proper apology and explanation, including a remedy that assures people it won't happen again. If the events that prompted the crisis were out of your control, if fate simply has conspired against you, then it is easier to recover your reputation by communicating effectively. Still, many companies with the resources to manage a public crisis don't do it well, which is why they end up digging a deeper hole. Either way, savvy leaders appreciate how essential it is to manage communication through a crisis and take steps to make sure it is done.

WHAT IS YOUR BRAND REPUTATION WORTH?

What is a reputation worth? Did just Tiger Woods's formidable golf winnings and hefty endorsement income get hammered? Actually, no. The companies that endorsed him also tarnished their brands, at least temporarily, as evidenced by the losses they took on their stock prices. Woods wasn't CEO; but he was a paid spokesperson, someone held up as symbolizing each company's values. The hit to his reputation had a tangible, negative impact you could measure.

As a brand champion, the CEO is in a unique position. He or she can either enhance respect for the institution or damage it. As CEO, you can either bring greater credibility to the brand or you can hurt it. In a public company, damage to your reputation can have an immediate and precipitously negative impact on the company's valuation. And sometimes that works in reverse. If you're working for a company that is not aligned with your values, it can sully your CEO brand.

Because your own brand reputation is so valuable, and so directly tied to the corporate value, you need to protect it. That includes doing the right thing, quickly jumping in to manage a crisis, and having a good team including public relations. Once a crisis happens, it is too late to go looking for someone to help.

At the same time, remember that PR is not a magic pill. There is no substitute for doing the right thing. No amount of press releases or paid media can erase an egregious, reputation-busting action. All you can do is take steps to avoid allowing it to spin out of control. The best insurance is to guard your reputation and your company's reputation with every fiber of your being, by making sure that you and your company are living by your values.

Stories of brand disasters are easy to find. Just go to the *Wall Street Journal*, your local newspaper, or any business publication. In this chapter, I've analyzed seven events that could have gone either way, explaining why some were failures and others successes. I hope these will provide useful guidelines as to what to do, and not do, when there is a crisis.

Let's begin with a success story.

IF IT'S BROKEN, FIX IT FAST—BOB ECKERT, CEO, MATTEL

Bob Eckert, the chairman and CEO of Mattel, has publicly said he will never forget the way he spent his fifty-third birthday, on August 14, 2008. He sat in front of a television camera in a conference room in Mattel's headquarters in El Segundo, California, delivering the same bad news over and over. Mattel was recalling more than 18 million toys, the most in company history, because of lead paint and design flaws, and there could be more recalls to come.

Employees interviewed in the media indicated that the message Eckert delivered both to the public and to them was the same. His e-mails, phone calls, and meetings emphasized one message: no matter what the impact on the company's revenues, safety comes first. Mattel committed to fixing the toy problems and protecting children's safety no matter what. According to news reports, Eckert, a father of four, told his employees that Mattel would be a better company in the long run.

BRAND DISASTER TOOLKIT STRATEGY NO. 1

Apologize quickly. Demonstrate that you mean it.

After the recall, Eckert reflected in *Fortune* magazine on why the company had not only weathered the storm but saw morale climb through the crisis. "All around the world, we apologized to parents," he told the magazine. "These were global recalls, and whenever we had the opportunity, we wanted to apologize to parents and that included parents in China." Eckert also apologized to the Chinese manufacturers who had taken the brunt of criticism for manufacturing errors that were not their responsibility.

In other media stories, Mattel employees corroborated Eckert's view. Deborah Dicochea, the associate manager of the Mattel Children's Foundation, said, "If anything, I think morale is even better than before the recalls. People are proud to say they work here, even through these recalls. We've come together as a family." Jeff Miller, a regional marketing director for Asia, said, "There was such conviction with everybody and such conviction from the chairman about what we were about to take on. You became part of a movement."

If you work in business long enough, crisis will test you. Whatever your business or industry, things can and do go wrong. The impact on your brand is determined by one overarching factor: how you respond. You either react in a way that shows you and your company at your best or in a way that shows you at your worst. If the response is weak, defensive, or arrogant, the reputational damage will be far reaching and impossible to control. If, as in Mattel's case, you handle it swiftly and adeptly, the damage will be minor, and you'll come out of it a better company. It's rare to see, but many companies actually improve their image because of the way they handle crisis.

Eckert was asked whether he feared for his job through the dark hours of the crisis. "My focus was always on what's the right thing to do," he responded. "I was not focused on my job. I thought about it in the company's terms: what's in the best interests of the company?" Eckert said the experience reinforced his belief that if you can consistently try to do the right thing, life is so much easier: "If you live by your basic values you'll get through it and you'll feel satisfied that you did the best you could."

THE SPILL AFTER THE SPILL—BRITISH PETROLEUM'S TONY HAYWARD

Press Release date: July 27, 2010

BP today announced that, by mutual agreement with the BP board, Tony Hayward is to step down as group chief executive with effect from October 1, 2010. He will be succeeded as of that date by fellow executive director Robert Dudley.

By the time British Petroleum (BP) announced the resignation of CEO Tony Hayward, he was already public enemy number one. Hayward had been vilified as the face of the oil spill in the Gulf of Mexico. His words were only digging him a deeper hole. After the explosion on April 1, 2010 on the oil rig *Deepwater Horizon*, which killed 11 people and unleashed the worst oil-spill disaster in U.S. history, Hayward's downward spiral was well documented. "Sometimes," a stunned Hayward told *Bloomberg Businessweek* (July 28, 2010), "you step off the pavement and you get hit by a bus."

Yet this was hardly a matter of chance.

Someday, as they write the case studies, authors won't be able to ignore the classic "secondary crisis," brought on by BP's incredibly inept handling of the situation. Arrogance did worse damage than the three-month spill itself. Hayward was a walking disaster. Early on, he predicted the environmental impact was likely to be "very, very modest." Later, he quipped that he would "like his life back." He took time off to go yacht racing with his son while Gulf Coast fishermen wondered whether they'd ever be able to fish and support their families again. After millions of gallons of oil tarred beaches from Texas to Florida, it was difficult to see Hayward as anything but detached, clueless, out of touch, and unrepentant about the incident.

Speaking to the U.S. House Committee on Energy and Commerce, he proffered an unapologetic defense, which only made lawmakers angrier. He positioned BP as a "model of corporate responsibility, taking steps that most other companies could not have contemplated, let alone done." He would not have changed what BP had done or the role he had played. One committee member accused Hayward of "kicking the can down the road."

To make matters much worse, allegations were surfacing that BP had lobbied for the release of Lockerbie bomber Abdel Basset al-Megrahi to help it win oil contracts in Libya. The public now saw the specter of BP helping to free a terrorist in the pursuit of profit. Hayward declined to attend the next hearing on that subject. "I have a busy week, so we are sending someone else," he said.

When you analyze the events as reported in the media, you don't have to look far to get the drift. The mistakes went on and on. BP was unprepared. Even worst-case scenarios can turn out well if you take responsibility and ownership. To not do so only makes people angrier. That's why you need a plan, a good team, and training for crisis management, including media. If you mess things up, it can take years to win back the trust of customers and the public.

BRAND DISASTER TOOLKIT STRATEGY NO. 2

Arrogance is the biggest brand killer of all.

People are willing to forgive almost anything except arrogance. That is what made Hayward's demise inevitable. His behavior cast a long shadow over BP. The millions spent on advertising to shore up the company's image was a waste. Commercials depicting BP employees on the beaches talking about their commitment would be dismissed as "bought and paid for." No amount of money would spin a positive story.

Hayward previously had a good reputation for bringing laserlike focus on safety. That legacy was lost. He wasn't helped by BP's chairman, Carl-Henric Svanberg, who after being summoned to the White House, referred to the victims of the disaster as "the small people."

If you are lucky enough to sit in the corner office, fly on the corporate jet, and play golf at the nicest country clubs, you must cultivate an attitude of gratitude and respect. Arrogance never works. You need people around to help, to tell the truth, and to help you get real when bad things happen.

NO OFFICE SECRETS—HEWLETT-PACKARD'S MARK HURD

Jodie Fisher, an actress who made a career appearing in R-rated movies and on the NBC reality show *Age of Love*, may never have imagined her résumé would include bringing down a major CEO. But it happened August 6, 2010, when her ties to Hewlett-Packard (HP) CEO Mark Hurd were exposed, and HP's board of directors forced him to resign. This was astounding since Hurd was so highly regarded. *Forbes* magazine had him at number 16 on the list of the Top 25 Most Powerful People in Business.

What tipped the house of cards was a letter Fisher wrote to the company claiming sexual harassment. The board investigated, concluding there had been no harassment but there definitely was a problem. They said Hurd had violated company policy by falsifying expense reports. What was he making payments for? They didn't know. Hurd had concealed his relationship with Ms. Fisher.

The glare of the spotlight grew harsher as Hurd was reported to have been creating phony expense reports at the same time he was ordering massive expense reductions to get the company on track. According to the *Wall Street Journal*, in an article August 8, 2010, Hurd had actually *championed* HP's written standards of business, stating that employees should pose a simple test as they decide whether an action is appropriate. That document states "Before I make a decision, I consider how it would look in a news story." The situation was particularly painful for HP because Hurd had galvanized the company through tough times. He oversaw one of the most successful corporate turnarounds in American business history. Under Hurd's leadership, HP posted five years of blistering profit growth and iron-fisted cost cutting. The stock outperformed the broader market by 101 percent over his five-year tenure.

Barrels of ink have been spilled telling the stories of the mighty who have fallen because they were engaged in unethical conduct. To err is human, but one thing every leader must know is that there are no secrets. Hurd's was a classic, self-inflicted wound.

He landed on his feet. In an ironic twist, he was hired by Oracle to replace Charles Phillips, who, according to published reports, resigned after an extramarital affair was made public on the Internet and billboards in New York. As for HP? Shares fell 8 percent on August 9, 2010, closing at $42.60, erasing $8.7 billion in market value. The fallout continued as shareholders reportedly lost $14 billion, or 15 percent of their "pre-sacking wealth."

Hurd would have done well to follow his own advice. He got his next job, but he managed to ding HP's brand.

GOOD THINGS FROM NOT-SO-GOOD THINGS—MARTHA STEWARD LIVING OMNIMEDIA FOUNDER MARTHA STEWART

Martha Stewart is perhaps the most prominent businesswoman of our time. When she was indicted for lying to investigators about a stock sale, she was a successful magazine publisher, bestselling author, and daytime television personality. Her programs were broadcast all over the world. Her empire encompassed thousands of home furnishing and other products, sold through partnerships with companies such as Sears and Macy's.

BRAND DISASTER TOOLKIT STRATEGY NO. 3

Imagine how it will look on the front page of the *Wall Street Journal*.

In 2004, when Stewart walked into a West Virginia federal prison camp to serve her sentence, there was rampant speculation about the future of her company. I recall doing several interviews with the media myself, about whether a company so closely tied to its founder and namesake could survive.

By her own estimate, Stewart lost about $1 billion. She told the media, "When you are prosecuted in such a way, a great deal of wealth is dissipated, and all I can think is what I could have done with all that for the good of mankind . . . I hope I can continue." she says.

What was remarkable was her comeback.

Upon her release in 2005, she hit the talk-show circuit. On the *Oprah Winfrey Show*, she shared stories of her time in prison. She was "delighted" when prison officials put her in charge of cleaning. With good humor, she said,

"I knew how to wax [floors]. That was easy," she told Oprah. "The hard part was learning how to clean the waxer. I had never really used a rug cleaner."

Stewart also championed the rights of the other 1,100 inmates, many of whom, she said, "had been there for years" and were "devoid of care, devoid of love, and devoid of family." She urged sentencing guideline reforms for nonviolent, first-time offenders. She posted letters on her website, thanking fans for their support.

Martha Steward Living Omnimedia returned to profitability the year after Stewart's release. She expanded her offerings at Kmart to a line of ready-made home furnishings. She announced new multiyear agreements with new partners for flooring products and wine. Her interior paint line became available at Sears. She published more books, and she became a contributor on the *Today Show* on NBC. Her talk show was nominated for six Daytime Emmy Awards.

When you start a company and name it after yourself, you must do everything in your power to protect your brand. No entrepreneur with his or her name on the door can afford to underestimate reputational risk. How did Martha Stewart manage to stem the loss and perhaps become more admired? She faced up to what she had done, did her time, and moved on. The public admired her for it.

BRAND DISASTER TOOLKIT STRATEGY NO. 4

Take your lumps and move on.

BRAND DOUBLE BOGIE—TIGER WOODS

If ever there were a case study in bungling crisis management, it was the first year after Tiger Woods's sordid, tangled personal affairs came to light. On his way to becoming the greatest golfer in the history of the game, Woods stumbled badly. From the moment he crashed his Cadillac Escalade at Thanksgiving, he couldn't get it right. As tawdry details about multiple affairs came to light, he was silent, then he lied, and then no one believed him. His golden reputation went into a freefall. The drip-drip-drip of bad news became a downpour.

Sponsors pulled TV commercials and print ads, although at first it was painful. Woods was the most powerful endorser on the planet with sponsors who collectively paid about $100 million a year according to Reuters. But the story was so big, and so out of sync with the carefully constructed, disciplined, family-man reputation Woods had built, that his image finally fell apart. This wasn't just any athlete caught in the cross-hairs. Woods's brand was "perfection," helping him become the highest-paid and best-known sportsman in the world.

What went wrong? So many things. With his global empire in chaos, Woods first tried to plead for privacy, issuing a statement on his own website on November 29, 2009, that read, "the many false, unfounded and malicious rumors that are circulating about my family and me are irresponsible." Then, he changed his story, issuing another statement in December, quoted by Reuters: "I have let my family down and I regret those transgressions with all of my heart." Yet the public remained skeptical. The apology didn't ring true. And then the women started appearing with their stories of extramarital affairs.

BRAND DISASTER TOOLKIT STRATEGY NO. 5

Tell the truth. It will come out anyway.

Throughout those early months it appeared that he had no one to speak the truth or that he had refused to listen to the rumors. This kind of thing isn't uncommon among powerful people. It is in fact, their Achilles' heel. The carefully controlled life Woods had constructed spun out of control without anyone there to help.

Woods's wife Elin Nordegren divorced him. By early 2011, Procter & Gamble did not renew their contracts with Woods. Endorsements with Accenture and AT&T, reportedly worth $35 million, were gone. Nike stood by him. But the damage was done. Eventually Woods became golf-focused, the hubbub quieted, and the public didn't care so much. He became a curiosity. It remains a mystery whether or not he can make a comeback. But you have to wonder what might have happened had he just come clean early on.

MORE THAN A FIX-IT PROJECT—HOME DEPOT'S ROBERT NARDELLI

In 2000, Robert Nardelli was a top-three finalist to replace Jack Welch at General Electric, the most-anticipated CEO changing of the guard in American business history. When he lost the job to Jeffrey Immelt, Nardelli weighed offers and chose Home Depot, which was growing faster than any retailer in history, even Wal-Mart. Somehow, Nardelli managed to mess it up. In spite of his initial success, he eventually destroyed his brand with employees, customers, shareholders, and even the public, becoming a symbol of greed, arrogance, and extravagance.

Riding the wave of the housing and home improvement boom in the early 2000s, Nardelli oversaw the growth of sales from $46 billion in 2000 to $81.5 billion in 2005, an average annual growth of 12 percent, with profits doubling that year to $5.8 billion, according to Bloomberg Businessweek. Then a housing slowdown brought declining store sales, which could have been dismissed as unavoidable, except that archrival Lowe's Companies' results were soaring. Its stock price was up—more than 200 percent.

Nardelli had a hard-line, numbers approach. At one time, Home Depot was a folksy, down-home retailer. Its founders had created a culture of "loving the customer." Nardelli poured $1 billion into new technology such as unmanned, self-checkout aisles. So while the company generated reams of data to measure everything that happened, what it didn't measure was the disconnect with customers. Accustomed to friendly service, they couldn't find anybody in the store to help them.

Nardelli provoked investors as well. He enraged shareholders who were expecting a routine corporate presentation, including time for questions. Citing time constraints and the imperative of working on important matters back home, the board "didn't show up at their own event," according to reports published by MSNBC, and therefore, Nardelli limiting the questions to one each, ended the comment period at 30 minutes. Shareholders declared war.

The final nail in the coffin was Nardelli's public negotiation to win a whopping compensation package. As Home Depot's stock was stagnant, he was collecting $124 million, not including stock options. In the background, Home Depot was among 200 companies caught backdating stock options, prior to Nardelli's arrival. He was cleared of any wrongdoing associated with this matter, but shareholders were now out for his dismissal. The board tried to trim his pay, with no luck. So they finally said good-bye. On his way out the door, Nardelli negotiated a jaw-dropping $210 million retirement package. Published reports said that after Nardelli's termination employees were texting each other with smiley-face symbols.

BRAND DISASTER TOOLKIT STRATEGY NO. 6

A dose of humility is a good thing.

Had Nardelli been judged on the numbers only, his job might have been safe. His metrics-driven leadership might have been seen as an overall positive thing. But the biggest issue was his loss of perspective, widely reported in the media as a product of arrogance. Disregarding critics cost him his job and his reputation.

THE COVER-UP IS THE SIN—MEG WHITMAN'S "NANNY-GATE"

Politics is a rough-and-tumble game. Businesspeople who enter the political arena often get bruised. You can earn your stripes on the corporate battlefield and still be unprepared for a political campaign. Such was the case when Meg Whitman ran as the Republican candidate for California governor in 2010.

When Gloria Allred called in the TV cameras and her client, Nicky Diaz, came forward with a tearful complaint, there was a healthy amount of skepticism about her claims of mistreatment when she nannied for Meg Whitman and her husband. With the news breaking a month before the election, Whitman's staff pointed out that Allred was buddies with Democratic candidate Jerry Brown.

Things quickly deteriorated when it was discovered that Whitman's husband, Griffith Harsh IV, had apparently signed a document that showed he had been informed that the nanny's social security number didn't match her name.

Diaz claimed she was terminated in a "cruel and heartless way" in 2009 when she came forward to ask the candidate and her husband for help obtaining U.S. citizenship. Her story about spending nine years shuttling the couple's kids around, doing extra chores, and cleaning up their 3,700-square-foot home was a headline grabber.

It wasn't the first time Whitman had been accused of employee mistreatment. She reportedly paid a $200,000 settlement to Young Mi Kim, one of Whitman's former employees when she was CEO of eBay, after allegedly cursing the young woman and shoving her in a conference room.

Whitman lost the election. What was interesting was that "Nannygate" wasn't the only reason cited. Whitman had reportedly spent close to $175 million of the money she amassed running eBay, one of the biggest Internet start-up companies to come out of the 1990s, on a losing campaign. While many political candidates spend their fortunes this way, Whitman's willingness to throw money at the campaign was perceived as out of sync with her promise to bring fiscal accountability and cut spending. As a result, many critics thought she snatched defeat from the jaws of victory. "Meg Whitman had the kind of resources most candidates only dream of, and she was a political outsider in the quintessential anti-incumbent year," said Arnold Steinberg in an op-ed piece in the Los Angeles Times, November 4, 2010.

The issue proved something that is always true for leaders in politics and business: if you fail to build goodwill, any issue can bring you down. Whitman hadn't built trust with the voters to begin with, so when Diaz showed up on the scene, the gubernatorial candidate was unable to fend off a challenge from an opponent who had been considered to be weak. It's hard to weather a crisis when you don't have a reservoir of trust already built up.

BRAND DISASTER TOOLKIT STRATEGY NO. 7

Without a reservoir of goodwill, one crisis will bring you down.

In the next chapter, we'll concentrate on how to build the team of people who help you build your brand.

CHAPTER SUMMARY

- Protect your leader brand like it is gold.
- Apologize quickly, and demonstrate you mean it.
- Arrogance is the biggest brand killer of all.
- Imagine how the news will look on the front page of the *Wall Street Journal*.
- Take your lumps, and move on.
- Tell the truth. It will come out anyway.
- When the storm starts brewing, don't just keep sailing in the same direction.
- Without a reservoir of goodwill, one crisis will bring you down.

Your Personal Brand Team— People Who Make You Look Good

We are no doubt in the great age of the brand.

—TOM PETERS

NOW COMES THE FUN PART—finding people who will help you build your brand and make you look good. We all need a little help from the right people to make it happen. It's time to assemble a dynamic group; people who have your best interest at heart, are committed to you, care about you, like you, and appreciate what you want to accomplish. Too many CEOs and leaders do not have enough support in building their brands. You deserve to have a first-rate team to help you do this.

Now is a good time to stop, look around, and see who you have available for your brand team. Who is already working with you? Anyone? How would you assess the job they are doing so far? What is getting done? What isn't getting done? What other talent and support do you need? Corporate communications, public relations, and marketing are sometimes not found on the executive's team. Remarkably in some large companies there is no one supporting senior executive communications, except administrators or human resources. Communications should not be an afterthought. Executives who have first-rate communication teams know what a difference it makes when building a brand.

You can't afford to let communications take a back seat. Given all that you have learned in this book, it stands to reason that you need at least one, and maybe more people, to help you. Where do you find them? Sometimes they are right there in front of you, waiting for a chance to shine. I always suggest to our clients that they consider who in their organization has enthusiasm and untapped potential. If you don't have anyone like that, you'll need to hire. There is no shortage of expert advice out there, from executive coaches, to marketing, writing, PR and other consultants, investor relations firms, Web developers, social media experts, videographers, production companies, and so on.

Experts working side by side with you on building your brand must be partners in every sense of the word. They have to know you, understand your preferences, and be devoted to you, and be experts at what they do. You should have people who are highly capable in offering strategic advice, as well as tactical people who can execute. You need idea people, people who understand your business, and also people who know how to get things done. Since public relations, marketing, and related activities are not that easy to measure, you need to agree on goals, outcomes, timelines, and measurement of results.

TIPS ON HIRING AND OUTSOURCING

When hiring and outsourcing, it is a good idea to keep these tips in mind:

- In a large organization, you may have plenty of resources, but they may not be obvious to you at first. You may not find them in "traditional" communications roles. You may not even have a large group in corporate communications. But you may have people in other parts of the organization with strong communication skills—and they probably would love to help you.
- In a smaller company, you may have to go outside to fill the positions. It makes more sense to do so to get projects done without increasing your staff. When outsourcing, think about whether you want to work with that person, as you would an employee. It's always important select people whom you like, who like you, who fit into your business environment, get along with others,

and have a strong track record of success. Look at them as an extension of your employee group, and hire accordingly.

- If you are a global company, you need a global team of talented people with skills specific to your company; who understand and can operate in the various regions and cultures where you operate. There are many ways to build a global team, usually by combining people who live and work in that region with your corporate team. The importance of being able to communicate your brand and values globally cannot be underestimated.

Over the years, I've hired many partners to work with Bates Communications, on every aspect of brand, from public relations, graphics, PowerPoint presentations, online publishing, printing, social media, marketing collateral, photography, book proposals, editing, video production, podcasts, speaker pitching, and more. The strategy of outsourcing works well when you select the right partners, and also manage the projects closely. Our firm regards these valuable partners as part of our brand-building team, an extension of our organization. When you have the right people in place, you can feel comfortable trusting them to help you achieve your goals. In this chapter I offer advice from my own experience as a coach, as well as people I know on the inside who work behind the scenes to help the leaders in their companies build their brands. You will get advice from the people in the trenches, from executive communications to public relations. These inside tips should provide you with insights as to how to hire and work with your brand team.

THE A-TEAM—WHERE DO YOU FIND THEM?

My rule is: talented people are everywhere, and they are often just waiting to be recognized. If you haven't identified your A-Team, here are some places to go looking:

- You may know a junior person in your organization who is eager for a chance to prove herself. Perhaps she would like to help with your presentations or speaking engagements.

- Perhaps you have someone on your marketing team who is doing traditional work but is social media savvy. He could research and outline ideas for your blog or outline or edit your weekly e-mails to your team.
- You may have a well-connected salesperson in your organization who can introduce you to power players in the community or make introductions to get you onto a prestigious board. In a large company, being creative is not that difficult. There are a myriad of people with the desire and capabilities to help.
- In a smaller company, your best bet is to go outside and find the expert resources who can address specific needs. Become expert at finding outside resources. When you find them, treat them well. Success is about the chemistry as well as the talent.

JOHN GUENTHER, BNY MELLON—WHAT DO YOU LOOK FOR WHEN ASSEMBLING YOUR TEAM?

John Guenther didn't start in corporate communications at one of the largest, most successful banks. He started his career as a writer-in-training on one of the best-known, longest-running soaps, *As the World Turns*. And while he didn't stay long at the job, he says, "The skills I gained working for a soap opera writer turned out to be invaluable."

Guenther took a temp job at Citibank, which ultimately led to a position in marketing communications at the Bank of New York (BNY). One day, he got a request to write a speech for the chief executive. He did it so well that the position became permanent, and he has now managed executive communications for the combined BNY Mellon.

The job goes far beyond speechwriting.

Guenther is the go-to guy on key messaging for the company, strategically managing all CEO communications as well as coaching other leaders.

Yet, he still regards the soaps as one of his most valuable experiences. He learned to write for the individual character's voice, a critical skill. He can now write for the leader, using his or her voice, cadence, words, and phrases, all key to making it authentic. He has also learned the art of telling the story. That may have been most valuable of all. In the corporate executive world, "It's all about storytelling," he observes.

"Communications has changed incredibly," says Guenther. Today, he says, employees of the next generation demand authenticity. They want to read or hear directly from the CEO or leader. They aren't as responsive to authority. They expect to be able to reach out and touch the leader.

A good communications person will make sure that you communicate in an authentic way. For example, when Guenther began working with CEO Bob Kelly, he noted his style was informal. "I saw the way he used humor and kept people on the edge of their seats," he recalls, "and I thought, we have to harness that."

This was a change from the buttoned-up culture of financial services. But it worked. "We started using a lot of humor, making it informal, and the feedback was immediately astounding," says Guenther.

Writing in *Your* Voice

"There is a big misconception that people like me put words in the leader's mouth," says Guenther. "I suppose some people do that, but it's always obvious, and it's never effective."

> "There is a big misconception that people like me put words in the leader's mouth," says Guenther. "I suppose some people do that, but it's always obvious, and it's never effective."

The best way to work is to develop a close relationship that allows the communications expert to write in "your voice." CEO Kelly has an internal blog that is based on the copious notes he takes while traveling. Guenther puts them into narrative form. After three years, the work is easy. They are a team.

The writing style is informal, just like Kelly's speaking style. The personal stories get the best response. Once he shared a story about growing up in Canada, where his family owned a luggage store. He challenged employees to be the first to stop by and send him their photo in front of the store. It happened within a week. "That's when we knew we had something big," says Guenther. "Now, whenever Bob is visiting staff around the globe, people always say, 'I love your blog.'"

As your eyes and ears, your communications team can be looking for examples and stories that illustrate the values and principles you want to drive home. You cannot be everywhere, but they can. Encourage them to go out and find material that you can think about and write about. They should help you gather stories that highlight great work, give credit where it is due, and reinforce brand messages.

Setting the Ground Rules

A brand team is a partnership, so when you ask team members to be your eyes and ears, you need to be open to what they tell you, good news or bad. If you trust them, as you must, they will help you build a powerful, authentic leadership brand. Set the ground rules, and let them know you want them to be observant, articulate, and courageous.

Encourage them to speak up and tell it like it is. If you find trusted communications partners, you can relax in the knowledge that they are going to support you. You may not always agree with them, but debate is a good thing. Listen, digest, and then decide. "There are a lot of leaders who just aren't going to embrace that," says Guenther.

Here's some advice on how to have a trusted relationship:

- Build it on mutual respect. People should adapt to your preferences and style, but your part is to open up so they can get to know you.
- Set the expectation that they will be in the inner circle, and allow them to understand how you think and what you really need.
- Spend time together, so they are able to capture your ideas and words, your way. If you want them to write in your voice you have to spend time with them and provide them direction.

- The worst thing you can do is send communications people off to write in their cubicles, divorced of your ideas and views. They can't produce you in a vacuum.
- If you're having trouble finding time to communicate, have communications people travel with you by car or even by plane, when you can get time one-on-one.
- When you come across information or have an inspiration, send it to the communications team immediately. Ask for brief responses, and give them the latitude to run with a timely idea quickly.

When you get together, let the people who are helping you ask questions and record the conversation. Their goal in writing should be to have the communication sound like your "voice."

In coaching, we use this process with tremendous success. Follow it and you'll move rapidly through drafts of a speech, video, or talking points for a media interview with better results.

Your team needs to understand the scripting and notes style you prefer. Whether what's needed are reference bullet points for an investor call or a formal speech that's scripted for a teleprompter, team members should manage it all. Be open to trying new approaches. Master every type of communication. Work with the team to help you make the communication compelling, conversational, and authentic.

WORKING WITH AN EXECUTIVE COACH

What can a coach help you do? If you're new to public speaking, a coach can work with you and your team on everything, from content development to platform style and skill. It takes time to develop skill, and sometimes while you have good writers on your team, they aren't speakers who can coach you on presentation.

It takes experience and good coaching to master the medium, whether it is video or big stage productions. A coach can help you with all that, and more. Perhaps more important, if you are writing stories—the ones that highlight your leadership brand—the right coach, with this expertise, can be a phenomenal resource.

Finding the Right Coach

Recently, one of the senior executive coaches on my company's team told us his client had been promoted to president of a Fortune 100 company, as the precursor to being named CEO in two years. This outcome had not been guaranteed. When our coach started working with the client, there were questions from the board of directors about whether this man was "the one" for the job. The issue wasn't his business acumen, or even his brand or "fit." In this particular case, he just needed to walk, talk, and project the CEO image. Board members needed to "see him as the next chief executive."

The executive worked diligently in the coaching program on board presentations. He developed more clarity about his brand values. He became adept at presenting his ideas in a clear, concise way. And he worked on his executive image. It was noticed.

The coaching relationship was essential to helping this individual rapidly achieve his goals. When you meet a coach who is skilled and dedicated to your success, you should grab the opportunity. A good coach will be forthright about what you need to do to move quickly toward your objectives. At Bates Communications, those certified to teach our tools and strategies have many years of experience both coaching and leading. That type of experience is what you should look for in a coach—not just someone who knows how to do things, but someone who has been there and done it.

A great coach is a partner in every sense of the word. As that person helps you develop skill, you should see results. A good coaching program should be a transformative experience. You owe it to yourself to give yourself this gift as you build your brand.

What If You Don't Have a Speechwriter?

Another situation where coaching can support you is with speechwriting. In my company, we "write with our clients." We prepare materials quickly by asking questions and capturing a person's words his or her way.

Surprisingly, even large companies often don't have professional speechwriters or communications experts in-house. Sometimes, the job goes by default to investor relations or human resources. That's a mistake. If you're serious about communicating strategically and building your brand, you need experts—people with skill who are dedicated to this important work.

WORKING WITH YOUR INTERNAL TEAM

When you bring a new communications team member on board, you want to get the relationship off to a good start. Erika Dornaus had just joined Constant Contact when I sat down to interview her boss, CEO Gail Goodman. Erika had worked on both the agency and the corporate side of communications. She knew that success would depend on getting off on the right foot. "The biggest challenge for me," she says, "was to understand everything the company offered . . . how it came together, and how we were going to continue to grow as a company."

The more rapidly you can expose new team members to the business, the better. "Constant Contact is great," says Dornaus. "They do a full orientation the way I've never seen it done at any company." The comprehensive program kicks off with a presentation by the CEO. "You learn not just about what we do. Gail tells you where we have been, where we are going, and then the head of each department comes in to talk about their function or line of business."

In the first 90 days on the job, she made a point of sitting down with key people and asking a lot of questions. She queried the veterans about how things really worked. She spent a lot of time with the CEO, both at employee meetings and events. Accompanying her boss to a gala "gave me a great opportunity in a nonformal setting, to hear her talking with our customers," she recalls. "That gave me insight into how she likes to present her brand and the company brand."

"It gave me a great opportunity in a nonformal setting, to hear her talking with our customers," she recalls. "That gave me insight into how she likes to present her brand and the company brand."

ASSEMBLE YOUR TEAM

To get an idea of what type of team you want to assemble, ask yourself the following questions:

What is the strongest part of your communications right now?

- Marketing
- Public relations
- Investor relations
- Community/public affairs
- Speechwriting
- Events/corporate meetings/productions
- Crisis communications/legal/human resources support
- Presentation training
- Photography, videography
- Web and social media
- Executive coaching

What are the weakest links, and why?

_____

What would you be able to do if you had these capabilities?

_____

What positions can you fill or change to close these capability gaps?

_____

What outside resources should you retain to provide expertise you don't want to hire?

_____

How to Teach People Your Business

Erika Dornaus was perhaps better prepared than most for the business side of communication. She had earned her MBA in an evening program while working in a previous job, at a startup company, where she was quickly elevated to a strategic role.

It's somewhat unusual to find a communications team member with an MBA, and an advanced degree is not necessary. What you do need, however, are people with a high level of interest in, and sophistication about, business. I look for people who exhibit intellectual curiosity and rigor. They have to quickly grasp and be able to craft a business message.

If you don't believe that those people are already on your team, don't settle, because they are out there. If you are not in a position to add a staff position, get assistance from a communications consultant or executive coach. Your team should have the full complement of skills and savvy required to help you drive your leadership brand forward. A coach or consultant can also help you interview and hire the appropriate talent for your team.

Agency versus Corporate Experience

When choosing a new member of your communications, public relations, or marketing team, you may wonder whether it is better to have someone with agency experience, or someone whose experience is on the corporate side. People with corporate experience understand how to operate in a company environment, work with a CEO and senior team, and protect the company interests. At the same time, people who have agency experience have had to juggle many accounts, work under deadline pressure, and have learned to be quick, flexible, and responsive. You may find the ideal person is someone with both types of experience.

You may wonder whether you should hire brand team members who already know your industry. There is no question that can be an advantage especially in the early months when there is less time and effort required to acquaint them with your business. Still, I would not make industry experience the top criteria for such a hire. Smart people who are committed to your business can learn quickly and be very successful. And, there can be benefits to bringing in someone from the outside who doesn't accept some of the standard beliefs and practices. There are benefits to bringing in a fresh set of eyes and ears to look at your brand and your opportunities in a new way. If everybody on the team is already entrenched in your business, you will miss out on getting fresh perspectives.

Old Media, New Media

Whether or not you bring in outside experts, your team needs to be abreast of the latest technology and trends. If team members aren't familiar with new media, they need to learn, or you need to complement their skill set with another hire. If your company has not been active in new media and social, it is likely that your communications, PR, and marketing group are not up to speed. Encourage them to read, go to seminars, listen in on webinars, and go to conferences to bring back the latest ideas to you.

Let me share an example of why it is so important to stay up on the latest technology and trends, from my own business experience. We were considering converting our website to WordPress, an expensive proposition because of the time involved to change over. Our marketing director investigated a new service, HubSpot, which would give us more capabilities than we had were seeking, at a fraction of the cost of converting all of the copy and photos on our site to WordPress software.

We discovered with the new service, we would not only be able to easily add Web pages, write or change copy, and run new promotions, we would also be able to easily track who visited our site, and gain important information to help us build our e-mail list, understand the profile of our prospects and ultimately, land more business. This was all a result of the work of someone on our staff who went looking for an alternative to the technology we knew and understood. It proved to me that having a team with a learning mindset is essential to your brand-building success in this ever-changing world.

Any people at any age can take it upon themselves to learn and stay on the cutting edge of trends and technology. I think it is important to hire people who are naturally curious, interested in what's new, and committed to learning as part of their own career trajectory and self-development. It is important to make it possible for them to attend conferences and give them time to learn, whether that means listening to teleseminars, reading, or dialing in to webinars, where they can learn from other experts.

Trusted Relationships

Of course, technical expertise is most valuable when you value and trust the people on your team. The relationship between you and the brand/communications team has to be built on trust. "Gail has been very trusting of me from day one, which has been great," says Constant Contact's Erika Dornaus. "She's given me the benefit of the doubt." At the same time, Dornaus owns up when she doesn't know something and asks questions. "I'll say, 'Gail, you and I haven't spoken about this topic before, and I want to get your perspective before I make a decision and a recommendation.'"

Dornaus says that establishing a great working relationship with CEO Gail Goodman's administrative assistant was also important: "I got to know her and became a close coworker with her, so that we could look together at an opportunity that would be important for Gail, or figure out whether she might say she didn't need to do it."

Dornaus says trust is built through give and take, not pushing too hard or acting like she knows it all but taking on more responsibility when she can. "Gail trusts that I won't just wing it when I don't know," remarks Dornaus. "She knows I will ask the right question to be sure we do what's good for the company." As she gains traction, Dornaus has a better sense of which interviews or speeches are right for Goodman.

A huge part of building trust is listening to each other. "We all like to think we know how something should be done, but before you go in guns blazing, you need to ask questions," says Dornaus.

In addition, I would advise you to find people who also have an opinion. That is an area where you need to solicit advice. Whether those people are coaches, consultants, or members of your team, you want them to make the right decisions, which can mean they need to push back. "I try to have a strong rationale behind what I am doing," says Dornaus. "Then you tend to get more leeway, because people trust you're making the right decisions."

KARYL LEVINSON, FORRESTER RESEARCH—WORKING WITH A SAVVY CEO

Even a savvy, self-sufficient leader needs great people to help communicate and build his or her brand. Karyl Levinson of Forrester has the privilege of working for a CEO who embraces and fully understands the power of communication. She is there to help George Colony execute—from brainstorming ideas for the next speech, to producing company meetings, and thinking through strategic communication issues.

Levinson appreciates a boss who prides himself on doing it well. "George's communication instincts are right on the money," she says. Colony prefers not to start his early preparation with a blank sheet of paper, but instead to edit the ideas that Levinson and his researcher draft for him. They outline with bullet points and send the ideas to Colony to help start the process and get him thinking about what he wants to say.

> "If a CEO isn't strong in a certain area, I don't think you should pull that lever," says Levinson.

LEVERAGING YOUR TIME

I've had the opportunity to employ a similar technique with my own team at Bates Communications. I enjoy writing, so I blog several times a week and tweet at least once a day, sometimes more. So, as busy as my schedule is, I need help. Our consultants, marketing director, assistant, and PR team are all on the lookout for ideas. They e-mail and text me articles and links to videos and blogs every day. Even my family gets in on the act. This is a great help; a jumpstart with a big idea gets me thinking, which leverages my time well.

WHO ELSE BELONGS ON THE BRAND TEAM?

Thus far, the people I've talked about on your brand team have been subject matter experts, from marketing, to PR and IR and traditional communications. However, you can and should think of your brand team as just about everyone who represents your company, and you. David Pisor, chief executive of Elysian Hotel, has a broad definition of who is on the brand "team." It includes every single staff member of the luxury hotel, as well as vendors and even customers. All of them have the ability to communicate both his brand and his company's brand. "I try to speak with the staff every two weeks about a particular book I've read, or an experience I've had with a guest, and I'll ask them to share something with me," he says. "It's a pretty open format."

Everyone who works with you and represents you should be a a brand champion, both for you and your company. This can and should include the people who buy your products and services. For example, Pisor learned that Harris Bank in Chicago had been providing a majority of the mortgages for purchasers of condominiums at the Elysian. Though they had no formal business relationship, Pisor recalls, "I called the president of Harris Private Banking to say we want to do an event for you." Pisor invited residents to an exclusive cocktail party. The note said: "We're proud and pleased to host the president of Harris Bank. Our success is due in part to their unique lending program." This way, the residents of his luxury condominiums become part of the "brand team," of people who are talking up Elysian.

> The note said: "We're proud and pleased to host the president of Harris Bank. Our success is due in part to their unique lending program." This is how he leverages everyone into a "brand team," people who talk up Elysian.

That's a great model for all of us: leverage who you know, and that includes anyone who has had an experience with you and your brand. Many fans in your brand community would be very happy to talk about what they love about you and your company. Take good care of these relationships and you will build a great personal brand.

Pisor had a wealthy buyer who purchased an entire floor for $6.5 million to build a spectacular luxury apartment, and he planned to put $2 million into renovations. The buyer was unhappy when he discovered that before he could start, there were $30,000 in repairs on a list of things to do. Pisor took care of the bill, with pleasure, stating, "[That buyer] would now recommend me anywhere in the world."

Think about everyone you touch as a brand ambassador! That's powerful.

In the next chapter, we'll share 10 powerful tips to accelerate your brand-building process.

CHAPTER SUMMARY

- You deserve to have an A-Team of players enthusiastically committed to building your brand.
- Build a relationship with each team member based on mutual respect.
- There may be untapped talent in your organization, so look there first.
- Bring in outside coaches, consultants, and PR and IR agencies to do specialized work.
- Give people time to talk with you, understand your views, and know how you think.
- Prepare for each event by working together with your communications team, so they can capture your voice your way.
- The most successful leaders put communications at the top of their list.
- Successful leaders also think broadly about all the people who they can recruit as brand ambassadors.

(11)

Ten Fast-Track Tips to Accelerate Brand Building

A brand name is more than a word. It's the beginning

of a conversation.

—LEXICON

AT THIS POINT YOU SHOULD FEEL excited, energized, and ready to start building your brand. The sooner you do, the sooner you and your company will see the powerful, measurable benefits. Your brand will open doors. Your brand will differentiate you. Your brand will be a competitive advantage. It will create enormous value.

Whether you are the CEO, a C-level executive, or want to be one some day, it is not too early to fast-track brand building. You've started by reading the book. The next step is to create a plan and then, take action. A year or two from now when you look back, I hope you'll be saying, "Wow, I'm glad I made that investment. I'm happy I took the time to build my brand. I see how it has changed everything."

Let's get you on the fast track. It's time to move. Let's build a brand that takes you to the top of your profession or industry.

In this chapter, I offer 10 fast-track tips for brand building. One caveat: brand building isn't about hocus-pocus or phony maneuvering. No amount of public relations or marketing can *create* your brand—it can only build *recognition* of your brand. You are the core of the brand.

The strategies we discussed in previous chapters work. It is important to identify and communicate the values and principles that define the core of your brand. Once you are clear about who you are and you master the art of communicating your brand values, these fast-track strategies will accelerate brand awareness.

YOUR UNIQUE BRAND

A branding campaign will fail if it isn't based on what is real about you. The idea that you can manipulate your image is passé. It conjures up images of publicists paid handsomely to create a perfect public persona. You're not a blank canvas. You are an interesting person who has lived a life. You have your own unique personality and style. As you build your brand, the activities should feel authentic to you. Publicity or marketing that doesn't ring true will be rejected. Falsely created public facades crumble under scrutiny.

Leaders within the same industry, company, or association have unique brands. They bring different experiences, values, and public personas to their work. Just as competitive companies have distinct brands, so do leaders. One of the best ways to fast-track brand building is to embrace the uniqueness of your own brand.

Look at the two most successful NFL quarterbacks in the league today—Peyton Manning of the Indianapolis Colts and Tom Brady of the New England Patriots. Both of these athletes are widely admired. Both are record holders. Both are winners. Both transcend sports. People see them as competing for the same mantle—best quarterback. However, their personas couldn't be more different. Consider their press and their sponsors.

In 2011, Manning had eight major endorsement deals with companies like Gatorade, MasterCard, and Nabisco/Kraft (Oreo cookies), worth approximately $9 million annually. Brady had deals with Uggs, the cologne maker Stetson, Movado watches, and Audi.

Their brands reflect their personal philosophies and their personalities. Manning comes across as a quarterback "of the people," with a friendly, accessible persona and a goofy sense of humor. Brady exhibits the image of a super-cool, easy-going jet-setter, his brand burnished by fashionable clothes and a thousand-watt smile. Manning jokes in a mock interview in a TV commercial that he needs to get "more production" out of sports announcer Jim Nance. Brady strikes a GQ magazine–model pose in a print ad for a luxury watch. Two Hall of Fame–bound quarterbacks— two utterly distinct (and incredibly valuable) brands.

Your brand, likewise, is distinct. You have your story. You have your experiences. Only you can be *your* brand. Think about that. Do it your way. Communicate who you are.

WHY FAST-TRACK BRAND-BUILDING

American singer Eddy Cantor once said, "It takes 20 years to become an overnight success." It's true, and it can feel daunting to start working to build your brand. That's why I offer these fast-track tips. You are busy with your life and career. It is easy to put things off when you aren't sure where to start. However, building your brand is important, and it will bring value to your company. If you have a plan and seize opportunities, good things will happen.

You can leverage one brand-building event into many. One of my clients, an accomplished physician and public health expert, was invited to give a lecture at Harvard University. Prior to thinking about building her brand, she probably would have just gone ahead and given the speech. But she was beginning to understand that these opportunities don't come along all the time, and you have to take advantage of them. So she decided to do more than just give a speech and instead to leverage the opportunity.

This client is more than a physician and expert, she is a thought leader in public health policy. She thinks deeply about important issues, enjoys researching her topics, feels compelled to encourage a dialogue with others, and speaks very effectively to audiences large and small. She had an intriguing angle for the speech, one that could make news in her field, so it was worth promoting it. She called me to brainstorm about the topic and help her write her remarks. Using her basic outline and initial research, I asked her questions, and we wrote out loud, drawing on her knowledge, viewpoint, and experience. A clear, compelling theme for this speech emerged. We both became excited as we saw how it was all coming together.

She decided it was worthwhile to also bring in a public relations team. The team members sent out a press release and helped her draft an op-ed piece for a newspaper with large circulation. We requested that the university videotape the speech, so it could be posted to YouTube, We knew this would also help us to pitch her for future speaking opportunities. She planned to have the team go out to other meeting planners, with organizations that would be interested in her topic. The speech was so good, it could be the basis for several public policy articles and media interviews. These publicity opportunities are more than single events; they can be posted online and leveraged to build her credibility and visibility. So you see how one speech can become so much more; a leverage point that can translate into a campaign to build a formidable, thought-leader reputation.

> I'm a big believer in the concept of massive action. If you have a big goal, throw your heart and soul into it, set aggressive deadlines, and get it done.

By recognizing the opportunity, she put a powerful plan in motion. That's what happens when you stop to think about leverage. Take a single opportunity and turn it into a brand-accelerating activity. Imagine the possibilities you have on a regular basis to do this. Think about the branding power you have with a relatively modest investment of energy, time, and resources, which will make an immediate, significant, and long-lasting impact on your brand.

As Henry Ford once said, "There is no happiness except in the realization that we have accomplished something." Take it a step at a time. Evaluate what is most important. You've come this far. You've started the journey. Keep going, and put the pedal to the metal. You're already on your way.

"There is no happiness except in the realization that we have accomplished something."—Henry Ford

FAST-TRACK TIP NO. 1: TAKE MASSIVE ACTION

When my first book, *Speak Like a CEO*, was published, I worked with our publisher, PR, and marketing team to create a multipage plan that would promote the book and build a following. In 2005, social media networking and marketing were in their infancy. At that time, we focused primarily on traditional marketing and e-mail. We assembled a list of CEOs, leaders, authors, experts, and others we respected, mailed them copies of the book, and asked for their endorsements. We planned a one-day promotional event online. We provided an opportunity for other authors who wanted to promote books and products to make an offering to their fans if they purchased a book. The idea was to get the book into the hands of enough people to jump-start readership and then build momentum with speaking and media.

It was a massive undertaking, but the results were impressive. The book started getting traction. We assembled a huge list of organizations that might want to book me to speak and began to reach out to them. After landing these engagements, the speeches helped get me introduced to companies I otherwise wouldn't have known and allowed me to build a larger database of clients, prospects, friends, and supporters. Coming out of the television news industry, I had only a small database of clients before I wrote the book. The speaking engagements and ongoing book promotion became a significant vehicle for building my brand and the brand of Bates Communications.

There were many elements to our book promotion plan, and by executing the plan, my team at Bates and I realized the power of taking massive action. Today *Speak Like a CEO* is published in many languages and read all over the world. It's been printed many more times and remains a business bestseller in its category. I looked at this colossal effort as a worthy investment of time and money in my business. It paid off in countless ways; some I expected, and others I never imagined. It differentiated our firm, grew our client list, gave our consultants entrée with senior executives, and became the basis for new products and services, including our *Speak Like a CEO* Boot Camp, workbooks, and audio programs.

Define what massive action means to you. Determine who you want to reach and what you want to accomplish when you do. Make your goals specific (for example, writing a bestselling book or being president of your industry association). Analyze the audience, and determine the best way to reach them. Then look at the people you have on your team and what they can do to help you build your brand. If you don't have the right people on your team, who else do you need to hire? What outside resources will be required? Bring the team together, develop a plan, and commit yourself to massive action.

If you're going to invest time and resources anyway, you might as well accelerate the process and get it done faster. While brand building doesn't happen overnight, the more committed you are to massive action, the faster you'll see results. Your brand-building plan will develop as you go. Jump-start it out of the gate with brand-building activities that make sense based on your goals.

If you find yourself hanging back, wondering what to do, or whether this is worthwhile, I encourage you to consider a time when you weren't sure that you should make an expensive purchase, something you had wanted for a long time. Perhaps it was a great set of golf clubs, a new home, or a beautiful desk for your office. You thought about it a lot; you kept going back to window-shop, but somehow you just couldn't spend the money. You told yourself there were other priorities, that it could wait. Then, something changed. And it wasn't your financial situation. You realized that that life was short, you could afford it, and you really wanted it. And you felt great satisfaction, once you made the purchase. It was the right thing to do; not self-indulgent, but rather, a meaningful purchase that you enjoy because it brought a new dimension to life.

Investing in brand building is similar in that you have to believe you deserve it. Many leaders are reluctant to put any of the focus of brand building on their own brand. However, your brand drives value into the corporate brand. The investment you make is worthwhile. Think about what an asset you can be to your company. That makes it a no-brainer.

Building your brand is an investment in your future, and the future of your organization.

FAST-TRACK TIP NO. 2: LEVERAGE, LEVERAGE, LEVERAGE

Leverage has been a strategy for every successful marketing and branding campaign from the beginning of time. One speech, video, article, or event can be the catalyst for an entire campaign. Here are a few examples:

- You write a story for a speech. That story goes into your blog. It becomes the basis for a bylined magazine article on a topic connected to your leadership brand. The article is pitched to a business reporter, who interviews you for a major newspaper. A television reporter reads the article and invites you on her show.
- At speech on a hot industry topic is videotaped and uploaded to YouTube. You also post it on your blog. Employees and clients read it. The 10 tips in that blog post become the basis of a booklet. The booklet goes onto your website as a downloadable PDF. It is distributed at client events.
- You attend a client event and are invited to be on a panel discussion with other experts. You broadcast it internally to employees at your office. The recording is also made into a podcast and uploaded to iTunes. The panel topic is pitched to a major industry conference. The conference organizer asks for an article for its trade publication.
- You are receiving an award on behalf of the company. You send out press releases to trade, business, and local media. The local news media print up a story about you and the other recipients. The organization posts an article on its blog. You invite some of your clients to the event. You send the award around to the office with a note of congratulations to everyone who contributed to your success.
- You do a television interview. The interview is posted on the network's website and YouTube. The link is sent out to other reporters to pitch you as an industry expert on the topic. You're invited to do

more interviews. Those interviews lead to a request to speak at a major venue. You send out a news release about the speech. You create a white paper on the topic and make it available to your salespeople.

Get creative about how to repurpose what you do, to reach more people.

Repurposing is not only allowed, it is incredibly savvy. That is how you increase the return on your investment in marketing and branding. That is how you justify the time you spend. Let me give you an example from my business.

I write a blog a few times a week. Sometimes, the article takes no time at all to put together; sometimes I have to research the topic. Either way, I spend at least a couple of hours, maybe more, on the project.

The effort is well worth the time because my company selects some of those blogs to go out in its newsletter, *Thoughts for Tuesday*. The marketing director uses a service to send it to thousands of clients, prospects, and friends. I tweet to my Twitter followers to let them know a new article is posted.

The next step is to ask the company's publishing consultant and thought-leadership expert, Ken Lizotte, to edit the articles for a book and pitch it to publishers. If we are successful, the book will be sold on Amazon.com, BarnesandNoble.com, as well as the company's website and at events. Those articles will be the inspiration for podcasts uploaded to iTunes. I'll bring in a videographer to record three-minute video vignettes. The company's public relations firm, the Goodwin Group, will send links of the video vignettes to meeting planners who are looking for keynote speakers. And so it goes.

That's my approach. What will be yours? Look at everything you do—*everything*—as the start of a worthwhile campaign, and leverage, leverage, leverage what you do.

Leveraging your material is much easier when you have a great team around you. Your time is valuable, and you need their expert help.

You will have ideas. They should, also contribute their creativity and strategic brainpower. Accelerate momentum by marshaling the team around you to develop a branding activity campaign, and then repurpose everything you create.

FAST-TRACK TIP NO. 3: GET COMFORTABLE *BEING* A BRAND

Earlier in the book, I discussed how important it is to think of yourself as a brand. You are a leader with a reputation you can leverage. Barbara Lynch, the chef and businesswoman extraordinaire whom you met in Chapter 4, was like many leaders I've met; initially she wasn't the least bit comfortable being a brand. Her company was originally called Number 9 (after her first restaurant, No. 9 Park), and she worked for two years to decide on a new brand identity. Lynch says that "I finally had to admit to myself that I needed a comfort level with being the brand myself."

Today Lynch has embraced the idea of being the brand. That started when she worked up the courage to put her name on the company. Now, it is Barbara Lynch Gruppo, a more elegant, Italian way of saying "The Barbara Lynch Group." She says, "At first I felt intimidated, but then I thought: this is good. And by renaming it, we grew up a lot as a company."

Think of the commitment that founders of companies from Disney, Dow Chemical, and Estée Lauder to Anheuser-Busch, Archer Daniels Midland, and Campbell Soup had to building their own brands, and how that helped their companies flourish and prosper. They understood the value of their names to their companies—and so must you. Whether or not you founded the company, your name is tied to the corporate brand; you represent you, and also the company you lead.

When you think this way, it increases the importance of spending time on brand-building activities. No one is going to give you permission to think of yourself as a brand and leverage your name for the good of the company. You have to grant that permission to yourself. Consider this your invitation—start thinking of yourself as an important part of the brand. Embrace the idea that you are a brand.

FAST-TRACK TIP NO. 4: SHOW UP AND REPRESENT YOUR BRAND WELL

Every time you walk into a room, you make an impression. That impression needs to be in perfect alignment with your brand. To accelerate brand building, you have to show up in an impressive way. You need to have a strong presence, consistent with your beliefs and values. Leaders with strong brand know how to command the room, to work a room, and to let people know in a quiet but confident way that they are in charge. Matt Davis, Vice President of Global Public Affairs for The Dow Chemical Company, is a polished executive who understands this importance of showing up in a way that is consistent with your brand. He advises those who want top jobs to remember they are always in sight. "That's why it is important for our leaders to always be up," he says. "Every interaction has to have impact."

There will always be times when you don't have the energy or desire to go to a networking session (or other event). It's okay to choose the activities that are important to your business and career. You have to balance these activities with the rest of your job, as well as your personal life. You do need to show up often, though, to build a brand. If you are always making excuses for not attending meetings and business and social events, remind yourself why it matters. Find a way to enjoy each experience by engaging with people in a genuine, energetic way. Go out of your way to meet people who you want to know, to make it worth your while. Wherever you go—to employee meetings, industry conferences, client events, social events, or networking events—show up looking and feeling your best, representing your personal brand the best way you know how.

No one is going to give you permission. You have to give it to yourself. Consider this your invitation—start acting like, and embracing, the idea that you are a brand.

If you lead a large organization, you may not have enough opportunity to meet or interact with employees and customers. In a big organization, many employees, customers, vendors, and others see you only rarely. Some people will only meet you once in their lives. The interaction with you "will stay in people's minds until you see them the next time," Davis advises executives. He reminds himself of this when he travels globally to visit his team. "If I am grumpy or down, what will be in their mind until they see me in six months or a year? I don't want them to say, 'I'm not motivated to be part of his team.'"

You can't build a brand sitting in your office. You have to get out there. There is no substitute for shaking hands and making a personal connection. For example, the president of my company, David Casullo, recently was in New York and met a friend from his college days. They had played football together. David made the decision to go to lunch together rather than just talk by phone. They reconnected in a meaningful way. The friend offered to connect him to a few major clients. David was delighted. You never know how showing up will open a door and create new opportunity.

Once people have met you and seen you in action, they feel a stronger connection. It's the difference between going to a concert, and listening to music on your iPod. Once you've seen your favorite band or artist, the music on the iPod sounds so much better. You create the same good vibration when you meet people in person. They feel the connection.

FAST-TRACK TIP NO. 5: DO THE THINGS ONLY *YOU* CAN DO

Focus your time and energy on the most important activities that will build your brand; otherwise, you will get overwhelmed trying to do everything. Do what you do well, and let others do what they know how to do. Let me give you an example of how to focus your own time on the brand-building activities you do best, from my own experience.

I was enthusiastic about writing my book. I love writing, and no one else can write the book that has my name on the cover. But I can ask other people to help make it successful. The marketing director at my company can set up speaking engagements. She can create the landing page on the website. And, she can promote it, in all the ways we promote through social and traditional media. The public relations firm can pitch interviews. The publishing consultant can edit book excerpts for business publications and newspapers. The curriculum director can translate the lessons of this book into the company's program for clients. Do what you do best. Then, let them do what they do best. That's how you accelerate the process.

When you choose to focus your own time on what you do best, you accelerate brand building. The following are a few examples.

- Even though she's a chef extraordinaire, Barbara Lynch finally hired an executive chef. Why? She did it because cooking wouldn't grow her business. She needed to be the creative force. She now cooks when the spirit moves her, at her experimental kitchen called Stir. "I like coming in and tweaking things and fixing things and inspiring my team with new ideas and new foods," she explains. "I'm working on new products and figuring out what to do in the next five years. I'm so excited about what comes next."

- A client of my firm, the president of a large division of a company, wanted to raise her visibility through speaking engagements in her city. Instead of sitting down and taking time out of her busy day to make these calls (or never getting around to it), she gave a protégé some guidance. This individual was productive and enthusiastic—and soon the two had several engagements booked.

- Another client hired a talented writer to review the copious notes that came out of a working group assigned to a strategic initiative, a group that the client had chaired. The writer transformed those notes into an impressive white paper. That document was distributed to a prestigious industry group. It received numerous favorable comments, and it raised the client's thought-leadership profile significantly.

Your real value is in doing what only you can do. Getting trapped doing things that you're not good at doing is one of the greatest impediments to brand building.

Your calendar is a reflection of your priorities. You only have so much time. By putting these activities on your calendar, and keeping the appointments, you are keeping a promise to yourself.

Think of yourself as the chef in your own brand kitchen. What could you be mixing up and serving up if you just worked on the recipe and had people in the kitchen to cook, others to serve, and others to manage the restaurant? What could you do, every day, for one hour, that would be the secret ingredient in the recipe? *That's* what you should be doing. Figure out your role, and then surround yourself with the team that can make it happen.

FAST-TRACK TIP NO. 6: COLOR-CODE YOUR *PRIORITY PROJECTS*

As you determine what you do best, put that on the calendar. Color-code your priority projects. The only way to make sure those things get done is to put them on your schedule.

My calendar has a reminder twice a week to write my blog. That entry is color-coded red, as a task. In the beginning, that was an important tickler. Every time I saw the "code red," it got my attention. Eventually, writing the blog became a habit. I remembered to do it without looking at the calendar. I enjoyed it and made it a part of my morning routine.

That of course means you need to put priority activities first, not last, after you've filled up your schedule with meetings, phone calls, and events.

When people in my company work with executives in the coaching program, we start with the calendar, to be sure that priorities are in order. I recommend that you block out vacation time, personal time, family time, and then priority projects, including brand-building activities. If you have all those things on the calendar first, then it is easier to make them a priority. Meetings, calls, and events can be scheduled around them, rather than the other way around.

One thing is certain—you will never "find" time for this. You have to "make" time.

I have a neighbor who has never managed to put his vacation time on his calendar. For whatever reason, he and his family just don't get around to deciding what they want to do. Although spontaneity is great, when the time is not blocked off, work flows into every crevice of his calendar. As a result, he rarely takes enough vacation time. In some years, he takes almost none.

On the other hand, my friend and mentor Alan Weiss, author of *Million Dollar Consulting*, is a prolific writer, speaker, and consultant who plans at least 10 or 12 weeks of vacation a year. He puts the dates on the calendar in December before the new year even begins. He travels the world with his wife, Maria, sees his children and grandchildren frequently, and has ample time to attend to his business. He has written 40 books. That is not a misprint. His name is the biggest brand in management consulting today.

If your schedule is not your own, and you're working within an organizational structure where you do not have complete control of your calendar, one strategy for managing is to use these color codes to keep yourself honest and focused.

My calendar is color-coded very simply, this way:

- Green: external
- Blue: internal
- Yellow: phone
- Orange: personal
- Red: task

Brand-building activities can fall into such categories as external, internal, or task. Just make sure you get them on the schedule. You may find that you simply don't have enough time, once you start trying to schedule them. In that case, another strategy comes into play—letting certain things go, so you can focus on higher-value activities.

Colin Angle, founder of iRobot, hired a designer for that reason. He loved doing design work himself, and he was brilliant at it. However, it was not the best use of his time. "For example, I realized one day that I had no business doing 3-D graphics even though I love design," he says. "We hired a guy who could do it way better than I did. And then I just said, 'Well, I guess I'm not doing that anymore.'" Be willing to make yourself obsolete where you can find someone to do it just as well or better. Put your energy, creativity, and focus into what only you can do. And get that time on your calendar.

Coach your administrative assistant to be ruthless with your time and protect it like it is Fort Knox. Make sure he or she understands the priorities. Make sure, even if it is uncomfortable for some people, that all appointments and scheduling go through one person. If you don't have an extraordinary assistant, you deserve to have someone who is an A-player. Give that person the power and latitude to make decisions on your behalf, and communicate well with him or her, all the time. Your assistant should be apprised of your brand-building activities and know that they are a priority. He or she can work with other members of your team, whether in public relations, marketing, or another specialty, to be sure that you devote the right amount of time, at the right time, to the things you really want to do.

FAST-TRACK TIP NO. 7: GET PROS TO HELP YOU IMPROVE YOUR SKILLS

As you build your brand, you will find that you need to get comfortable giving speeches, presentations, and media interviews. These are not natural born skills; you learn through coaching, training, and experience. Learning these skills is just like learning how to do anything. For example, I do not play golf (yet). My husband says I will hate it and be frustrated; nevertheless, he and I have just joined a golf club. Now is the time. I want to learn to play. I can't just go out and hit the ball. I know that if I am going to learn I'll need to take lessons from a pro—someone who knows the game and is a good and patient teacher. And then I will need to play often. As much as I love him, my husband won't be my coach.

He plays golf, he's a patient man, but as he will tell you, coaching me is not a job for him. I need a coach with experience teaching novices like me how to play.

If you know this to be true about one skill (such as my golf), why wouldn't it be true about speaking, media, and others? Why would you book a keynote speech at a major industry conference and not get the coach to help you show up as the best you can be? A poorly crafted, lackluster speech is not a brand builder. The same is true of media interviews. These opportunities come along rarely in the beginning, but if you prove to be a good interview, the media will call again. Why wouldn't you get training in all the skills and strategies that will make you successful? When fast-tracking your brand, it isn't enough to get by; you need to develop a level of skill and confidence that represents you and your brand.

My company once had a client who was scheduled to work with the coach on a speech for a major industry event where a significant number of his company's target customers would be. This CEO was not a good speaker, and frankly, he wasn't that interested in becoming one. His marketing director was the one who called my company because he knew what was at stake. One day, when the coach arrived at the CEO's office, the executive came out and told her he didn't have time for the session, even though someone had called ahead to confirm the appointment.

The speech didn't go well. It was, as a matter of fact, a huge disappointment. Even the CEO realized afterward that he had blown a great opportunity. If you want to improve your "score" as a speaker, just as you might want to improve it in golf, you need to practice and spend time with a coach. One presentation course will not transform you into a great speaker.

Find a coach who is a pro and has the skill, dedication, and ability to make you the best you can be; then put yourself in her or his hands. A good coach should be able to help you do these things:

- Develop thought-leading concepts
- Help you write your stories
- Find the values and principles in them
- Think through your priority projects

- Schedule and keep those appointments
- Develop skills such as writing and speaking
- Find and work with resources such as public relations and marketing
- Videotape and help you practice speeches and interviews
- Outline ideas for published articles
- Help you prepare memos and e-mails to your team
- Assist you in planning themes and remarks for town halls and client events

That list isn't complete, but it should give you an idea of what you should ask of a great coaching partner.

FAST-TRACK TIP NO. 8: HELP OTHER PEOPLE GET WHAT THEY WANT

There is nothing so potent in brand building as doing favors for other people and helping them to get what they want. It's not just the right thing to do, it has many other benefits. People remember people who help them, and that fast-tracks your brand. Peter Shankman founded HARO (Help a Reporter Out), a public relations service that connects reporters with sources who want to share their expertise with the media. HARO is a brilliant invention. It helps both journalists and the experts who want to get media coverage. Shankman realized that he could help people make a connection through an electronic service. It caught on quickly. HARO's tagline is: "Everyone Is an Expert at Something."

What Peter Shankman had been doing was helping other people get what they want.

Before selling his business for a hefty sum, Shankman built an impressive client list that included Sprint, the Department of Defense, Walt Disney World, Abercrombie and Kent, and American Express. What's impressive is that he built a great business and a brand of his own. How did he do it?

"When you look at HARO," says Shankman, "I don't think it came across as massive *self-promotion*. HARO was designed to help people."

Shankman realized that the best way to build a name in business was to be there when he could, to provide advice or a favor.

For instance, he had a client who was married to a pilot at the National Aeronautics and Space Administration (NASA). She wanted to negotiate a lower fee for a HARO ad. She needed help to write it. Shankman did it at no cost. "A couple of months later," he remembers, "they invited me to visit NASA." On a tour, Shankman was introduced to a high-ranking NASA official. Eventually he was invited to join NASA's civilian board. "I didn't need to meet people for coffee," he jokes.

We all know how much power there is in helping other people. It attracts them to you and makes them want to help you, as well. They remember your generosity. They tell other people about you. They don't forget the favor you did for them. Helping other people is a fast-track brand-building activity, and you can also feel good about giving back.

As the imaginative Shankman says, "It's the difference between going to a bar and asking a girl to come home with you, and having a girl look at you and having your friend say, 'you should go home with him.'" When you help other people, they return the favor. There's no substitute for having one of your "fans" tell a client or prospect, "I know him, he's great."

FAST-TRACK TIP NO. 9: GIVE IT THE *PERSONAL TOUCH*

Everything around you is an extension of your brand, representing who you are and what you stand for. When there is harmony between your inner brand and your outer surroundings, it reinforces and fast-tracks your brand. For example, your stationery, clothing, and office are all a reflection of your brand. All of it should have a personal touch that says you. Everything around you should represent your brand well.

Your brand image is as distinct as you are. That means it should be personalized. At the same time, in corporate life, there are standards. The best way to stand out is to fit in perfectly and also give it your personal touch. I like to tell clients of my company, "If you want to wear cowboy boots, you live in Texas; and if it suits your business and lifestyle, do it." That's an authentic representation of your brand. It's a memorable "click," or connection, and it feels great. I don't recommend you wear cowboy boots to a board meeting simply because you got up one day and decided you like them. A sudden change like that in your style has the potential to create brand confusion, especially if you show up the following week sporting another look.

I'm not trying to stifle expression because individual style is an important part of your brand. It's fun to discover that style and express yourself and your brand through clothing, image, office, and surroundings. Be sure that your surroundings precisely reflect the brand image you want to project. This doesn't mean that you should follow the rules so closely that you come across as dull, too conservative, or unimaginative. If you know yourself, then you will know what looks and feels right and also represents your brand image. Surround yourself with the things you like, enjoy, and feel to be a part of you.

Everything you do should have your imprint. Everything you wear and everything that surrounds you represents your brand.

Most people have a style that evolves over time. That's a natural part of growing as a person and discovering who you are. Still, a consistent image is a fast-track brand builder. It gives people an image they can anchor in their minds when they think about you. Think of Steve Jobs in a black turtleneck and jeans, or Martha Stewart in slacks and a light-blue cotton button-down blouse; both signature looks capture them. They never stray from this image, and it works. It's brand-enhancing. I'm not suggesting that you need to wear the same clothing all the time, in fact, that would be gimmicky. However, when you know who you are and are mindful of making choices consistent with that, it reflects a strong, consistent brand image.

To fast-track the image aspect of your brand, I recommend getting some guidance. Hire a wardrobe consultant or find someone who is expert at image who can help you. Clean out your closet this weekend, and get rid of everything that doesn't suit your brand, your business, and your lifestyle.

Hire a designer or decorator for your office. Tell them what image you want to project. Allow them to use personal touches and also bring it all together for you. Have a great family photo taken by a professional photographer, and display it proudly in your office.

FAST-TRACK TIP NO. 10: ASK, WHAT DO I WANT TO DO THAT I HAVEN'T DONE YET?

That word *yet* is important. It implies you want to stretch and grow. Take a look at the list below. Some of these activities aren't glitzy, but they might be great ways to communicate and build your brand.

> What haven't you done yet, that you would like to do? Whatever is on your "list," it's time to put it in writing and ask yourself, "What haven't I done yet that I would like to do?"

Where do you want to be known? Where can your clients, employees, and important audiences find you? Look at these as places where you could leave your brand "stamp." What are you doing well? What aren't you doing yet that you'd like to do well?

- Media interviews (TV, radio, print)
- Industry speeches
- Sales meetings
- Client presentations
- International speaking
- Blogging
- Twitter
- Op-ed
- Newsletter for clients
- Byline articles
- Published books
- Booklet

- Facebook
- LinkedIn
- Podcast
- YouTube
- E-mail newsletter
- Webcasts
- Internal newsletters or blog
- Networking in business groups
- Member of prestigious clubs
- President of an organization
- Member of a board of directors
- Industry awards
- Member of policy-making groups
- Advisor to government officials
- Business leadership groups
- Other

PLANNING EXERCISE

As you sort through the options in the preceding list, ask yourself two questions: (1) What am I doing now that I love to do and can leverage even further if I put energy and resources into it?" and, (2) "What am I not doing yet but would love to do?" The reason you ask it this way is because there may be activities you feel you *should* engage in that you won't be able to sustain if you don't really want to.

Activities I Do Now and Enjoy Doing

1. _____
2. _____
3. _____
4. _____
5. _____
6. _____
7. _____

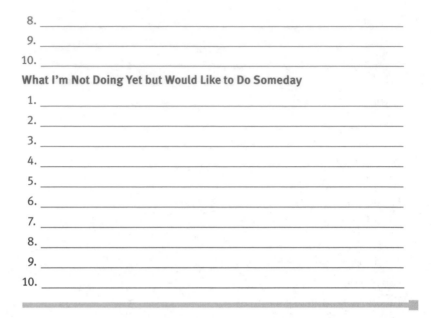

8. _____

9. _____

10. _____

What I'm Not Doing Yet but Would Like to Do Someday

1. _____

2. _____

3. _____

4. _____

5. _____

6. _____

7. _____

8. _____

9. _____

10. _____

By "would love to," what you're acknowledging is that the activities are not in your wheelhouse yet but could really resonate with your brand. They are a fit, and they could help you accelerate brand building in a way that makes sense. You and the people in your organization don't have to have the knowledge to do it yet, but you could gain that knowledge. You might enjoy it, find you're good at it, and set yourself apart from other brand leaders as a result.

One thing I learned over the years in deciding what to do and what not to do is that if you don't enjoy it, you won't sustain the effort. For example, I worked with several nonprofit organizations over my 20 years in television news. There was always an event to emcee, or a project to lend your name to, or a committee you could join. Many of those causes were well worth it, and the people I met were incredible. However, when I left and started my firm, I wanted to do a reset. I wanted to be sure that I gave my time to organizations that were important to me.

Eventually, I became president of a nonprofit board, and later, a professional association, and I worked with a number of other new organizations. The time you have available for these activities is limited, so you have to be sure they are aligned with your interests and, of course, your brand.

FINAL THOUGHT—INVEST IN YOUR SUCCESS

As president of my National Speakers Association New England chapter, I've met hundreds of experts who speak. A lot of them have written books but have been frustrated when they don't sell. "What am I doing wrong?" they wonder. The answer is—not enough. Without commitment, time, and tenacity, they end up disappointed with the results.

Investing in success is important for any leader. It takes effort to build a brand. You can accomplish a lot with a little, if you're smart and have a good team. A reasonable budget, well managed, will accelerate the pace. You'll be excited about the outcomes. You never remember precisely what you spent. You remember the great results you achieved.

In the next and final chapter, you'll find out ways to build your brand so others remember these results, too. That means creating your leadership legacy by writing history today.

CHAPTER SUMMARY

- Take massive action.
- Leverage, leverage, leverage.
- Get comfortable being a brand.
- Show up and represent your brand well.
- Do only things *you* can do.
- Color-code your priority projects.
- Get pros to help you improve skills.
- Help other people get what they want.
- Give it the personal touch.
- Ask: "What am I *not* doing yet, that I want to do?"

12

Your Leadership Legacy—Writing History Today

"How we spend our days, of course, is how we spend our lives."

—ANNIE DILLARD

AS YOU LOOK AHEAD TO THE rest of your career, I'd like to ask you to think about these questions: How will those days add up? What will these years in leadership mean? What in the end, will my legacy be?

Interestingly, when I posed these questions to leaders in this book, their answers about legacy came easily. They had thought about the purpose; they were clear about the importance of their work; they had thought about the difference they want to make. This direction and sense of purpose gives meaning to their everyday activities. Each time I asked this question of the leaders I interviewed, they were able to tell me with a mix of humility and pride, what they hoped their careers would be about. As they looked to the future, they were focused on where they still want to go and what they want to do next.

Building a brand is all part of the process of bringing meaning to our work and accomplishing great things. You are more influential when you have a powerful brand. You are able to reach more people and achieve bigger goals when people know and respect your reputation. Your brand attracts people and opportunity and allows you to drive value into your company.

You will feel a greater sense of satisfaction as you stand on a bigger stage and make a greater impact. At the end of your career you will be able to look back and see how exciting and rewarding it was. A strong leader brand allows you to do more for the organizations you had the privilege to lead.

As this book draws to a close, I hope you have already discovered some of the important elements of your leader brand. I hope that you've already written down stories from your life and career and reflected on your brand values. I hope that clarity will inspire you to communicate your brand values in a powerful way, and ultimately leave a legacy.

This book gives you the strategies and tools to build a powerful brand and use it to drive value into the organization you lead. You might say using these tools and building a brand is one of your obligations as a leader. Your team, your company, and your industry need high profile leaders like you to speak up on issues and represent them well. I hope that you will take this opportunity to formulate a brand plan, and direct your energy into raising your profile and leveraging it to the benefit of others.

As you build your brand, you will not only attract people and opportunity, you will be a role model to leaders in the organization. More and more, the corporate clients of Bates Communications are talking about how important it is for them to help their leaders tell their stories, share their values, and be models of good communication to up-and-coming leaders. We are working with them to discover and tell these stories and to help our client organizations shape a shared history through the stories of their leaders. As top executives prepare to retire and leave an organization, this is vital. The history of your company, and how you came by the values that define you, is perhaps the most important memory to keep alive and pass on.

What is a legacy? In essence, anything handed down from the past or a predecessor. Consider leaders in your life who you have admired. No doubt you remember what a difference they made to you in your career. They understood the importance of being a role model. They passed along the lessons and values to you and others. Today, you have that same opportunity, to become just such an influential leader, someone others admire, respect and want to emulate.

In the final pages of this book, I'd like to share some stories about leaders who are in the throes of writing their legacy. You'll find the stories of well-known leaders, juxtaposed with stories of leaders you met in this book. They are grouped into four categories: innovation, reinvention, people, and community.

If I were to write another book, I could include a thousand more stories, perhaps ten thousand more. Perhaps your story would be among them. I would love to share the story of your journey, the lessons learned, and how they have defined you as a leader. It would be a privilege to find out how you built a brand and had impact on your team, your company, your industry, and your community.

Your story isn't finished yet. You are writing it today. I hope that these final stories will motivate you to tell your story and build your brand.

INNOVATION

Some great leaders have built brands by championing innovation. Here are the stories of two leaders, one from the past, one from the present, who became known as innovators.

Henry Ford—Innovation for the Common Man

Henry Ford founded Ford Motor Company in 1903, with 11 other investors and $28,000 in capital. Born on a farm near Dearborn, Michigan, his dream was to build an automobile for the "common man." Ford's genius was realizing that with the right techniques, he could mass-produce cars. As the son of a farmer, he knew that making something that was cheap, reliable, and easy to maintain was just common sense.

He didn't invent the assembly line. He didn't even know at first how he would mass-produce the Model T. But when he figured it out, he was able to build it and price it at $850, a bargain compared to the $2,000 cost for most other autos selling at that time. Eventually the Model T's price would come down to $300, creating huge demand. By 1918, half the cars in America were built by Ford.

Henry Ford once said, "A bore is a person who opens his mouth and puts his feats into it." He may not have talked much about his legacy. However, his philosophy that the "common man" should be able to own an automobile revolutionized our world.

Colin Angle, CEO, iRobot—Writing a Legacy Today

Thinking back, Colin Angle considers his undergraduate thesis to be the first step in creating his vision. He set out to build the coolest robot he could imagine. "It was a walking robot named Phillip with 15 computers, all in an 18-inch-long package," he says. From that experience, he realized he wouldn't be able to re-create the popular cartoon *Jetsons*-type robot (one that looked like a maid and would cook food and fold his laundry), but he could make one that would touch people's lives daily.

"At my core, I think I am very practical," he says. "If I had been one of those blue-sky visionary sorts, I would have wanted to stay in academia and continued building robots that were amazing but not that useful. That wasn't me." iRobot entered and exited 18 different businesses, including a private mission to the moon and Roomba, the robotic vacuum cleaner.

"We changed how NASA approached space," says Angle. "We explored the great pyramid in Egypt. We were the first robot to be used ever by the U.S. military on a combat mission. And now with Roomba, we have 5 million vacuums that are changing the way people think about robots."

REINVENTION

Leaders also become known for reinventing the institutions they lead by looking at what needs to be done. Here are examples from the past and present of leaders whose brands are defined by reinvention.

Lou Gerstner, International Business Machines— Elephants Can Dance

Gerstner came to the International Business Machines (IBM) Company by way of American Express and RJR Nabisco, taking the helm at a time when the once-mighty company was gasping for air. No one thought that the core mainframe business would survive. The management team was disbanding and rebranding businesses as "Baby Blues," a term that described the companies that would be spun off in the reorganization."

Gerstner put a stop to that and created a plan to revitalize IBM as a broad-based integrator of technology. His controversial decision to hold the company together and focus on IT services wrote the story of one of the most remarkable turnarounds in American business history.

In his memoir, *Who Says Elephants Can't Dance?*, Gerstner described the wrenching decisions as painful, especially the layoff of 100,000 workers. It had to be done in a company where employees assumed they had lifetime employment. But he saved IBM and put it back on a path to greatness, ultimately creating jobs and an entirely new business. His legacy? Upon retirement, he wrote that IBM had become "a company that mattered."

Ellen Zane, Tufts Medical Center—Writing a Legacy Today

Ellen Zane of Tufts Medical Center didn't need a CEO job when Larry Bacow, president of Tufts University, called to ask her to assume that position. But Bacow shared the remarkable history of the hospital and what was at stake. The organization, founded by Paul Revere in 1796 with an outpatient facility for the poor, at the time of the phone call had 10 months of cash and was burning $4 million a month. It might not survive.

Zane had turned around Quincy Hospital and helped build Partners into one of the largest physician networks in the United States. Five thousand jobs were at stake, and Tufts Medical Center was an anchor for one of the most economically depressed areas of the city. Zane thought that if she ever wanted to do something important in her career, this was it. She saw what needed to be done. "I've had the ability to be bold when I have to, and that has been hugely helpful in a hard job."

What about a legacy? "That people's lives were changed, not by me alone, because we are only as good as people around us, but by virtue of the fact I chose to take on this challenge, is important," she says. "I want this organization to be here 200 more years. When you put the pieces together and know you're making a difference to employees, patients, and the community—that is gratifying."

PEOPLE

Some leaders build great companies through their commitment to people. Again, here are two examples, one past, one present, of leaders who can claim the word "people" as part of their brands.

Herb Kelleher, Southwest Airlines—Low Fares, Lots of Fun

Legend has it the business plan for Southwest Airlines was written on a cocktail napkin during a conversation between Herb Kelleher and Southwest Airlines cofounder Rollin King. In the 1960s, the highly regulated world of airlines was expensive; air travel was for businessmen and people with means. Southwest dared to avoid the hub-and-spoke model at large, congested airports. It forged a new business model with quick turnarounds and no meals.

Kelleher grew up in New Jersey. After his brother and his father, a Campbell Soup factory manager, died in World War II, he grew close to his mother. She was a working-class Irish woman who taught her children the importance of treating people with respect.

Southwest became famous not only for frugality and efficiency but also for its hard-working, fun-loving culture. Kelleher was well known for having a good time and giving great parties. Flight attendants sang songs; pilots cleaned cabins. Kelleher also built a culture of respect based on taking care of employees. Southwest was the first to offer profit sharing, with higher pay scales and better benefits than other airlines. Kelleher once sold an airplane rather than lay off employees. In 30 years the company never had an involuntary dismissal. His legacy is a low-cost business model combined with a high-spirited culture that many have admired, though few can replicate.

Lisa Matthews, Financial Planner—Writing a Legacy Today

When financial planner Lisa Matthews was growing up, she wanted to be, not necessarily in this order, an astronaut, a diplomat, and a minister. She realized early on she wouldn't qualify for NASA because she had claustrophobia and dizziness. "However, flying high became a metaphor, as my business soared higher than I could imagine, and I loved what I was doing every day." She started by helping her grandmother and aunt with their finances, and her business blossomed.

But she still was conflicted. When she and her husband went to see a priest before their wedding, she mentioned her thoughts about becoming a minister. "The priest looked at me and said, 'Aren't you a minister now?'"

Instead of going up in the air as an astronaut, or ministering to the congregation, she committed to educating her clients and helping them fly high to achieve their financial goals.

Matthews became passionate about the work, even though she battles epilepsy, cancer, and a painful joint disease. A doctor once told her that she was "the strongest-willed person he's ever met. He thought of having me consider disability and realized it would be the worst thing, because I love what I do."

She's writing a legacy with those she's trained—"over one hundred salespeople and advisors who worked with me in businesses, many who today have their own businesses as a result of what they learned." Her proudest achievements have been helping clients invest, to buy homes, retire, and pursue their dreams. She notes that "one of my clients introduced me to her son and said, 'This is Lisa Matthews, if it weren't for her, you wouldn't have gone to college.'"

COMMUNITY

Some leaders reputations extend beyond their companies because what they do has such an impact on the community or region. Here are examples of two such leaders, one from history, one from the present, who can claim community as part of their brands.

Daniel Burnham, Architect—Rebuilding Chicago after the Great Fire

From Sunday, October 8, to early Tuesday, October 10, 1871, the Great Chicago Fire burned, killing 300 people, destroying about four square miles of the city, and leaving 100,000 homeless. Out of the ashes of one of the largest disasters of the nineteenth century came Chicago's development into one of the most well-designed and vibrant cities in the world.

One of the Chicagoans who led the way was architect Daniel Burnham, who designed the first urban plan for a city, the 1909 Chicago plan. It was nicknamed "Paris on the Prairie" and featured the wide boulevards and parks that grace the city today.

Burnham and architect Frederick Law Olmsted were also behind the World's Colombian Exhibition in 1893, also known as the Chicago World's Fair. This fair made a profound impact on architecture and the arts and came to represent the dawn of American Industrial optimism.

As chairman of the McMillan Commission, Daniel Burnham helped develop a plan for Washington, D.C., that shaped the National Mall that we enjoy today. Burnham also developed city plans for Cleveland and San Francisco, as well as Manila and Baguio City in the Philippines.

After his death, Burnham's oft-quoted advice, "Make no little plans; they have no magic to stir men's blood," became the mantra for thinking big. Those who knew him agreed it captured his spirit, vision, and legacy.

Barbara Lynch, Barbara Lynch Gruppo— Writing a Legacy Today

It isn't about the glory of getting "best chef" awards for Barbara Lynch, though those are great. For the girl who grew up in the South Boston projects and dropped out of high school, it's much more. She's discovered a passion for creating career opportunities for people who work for her, and also giving back to the city where she was born and raised.

People often ask Lynch why she decided to expand her restaurants, when she already had several successes. Part of it is the outlet for creativity, as well as "a driving force to invest in employees," says one of her top people, Sarah Hearn. "She is such a visionary and has this unique talent."

Her restaurants have thrived as she schools new chefs, creates innovative new menus, and mentors people who want to make restaurants a career—because they love it as she does. "We just had our company Christmas party," she says, "Our first party was 30 employees. This time we had 400. It's crazy. It's amazing."

Lynch could have gone off, as many celebrated chefs have done, and opened restaurants around the country in, say, New York, Washington, or Las Vegas. She decided to stay in Boston, to be with her family, and invest back in the city. "I love when customers say thank you for making Boston a better city by adding wonderful restaurants," Lynch beams. "I could have gone to Vegas, but I think this is a great city; it's been great for me."

The Story of My Dad—A Small Town, a Big Legacy

One of the people who inspired me was my dad, Richard K. Bates. When I was in elementary school, my town voted against a much-needed school referendum. Without the additional tax dollars, difficult decisions were unavoidable. The school board slashed the budget, and teachers lost their jobs. The five junior high schools went on half-day schedules. Classes started at 7 a.m. and finished at noon so the afternoon students could occupy the same seats. I reveled in the lazy afternoons at home and wouldn't have paid much more attention except for one fact. At the time, my dad was president of the school board.

People were critical of my dad and the board. They forgot that their votes had created the financial chaos. Eventually dad and the board got the town through a challenging time. Budgets were restored. School life went back to normal. I was too young to know or appreciate all that happened. It wasn't until years later, when he died and I had to write his obituary, that I realized what his brand, and his legacy had been.

As I sat on the floor poring over a few tattered yellow clippings, I found a new appreciation for his difficulty. There were impossible choices, unhappy neighbors and friends, and an exhausting schedule of endless meetings. They stole significant time away from a family and a law practice that were both young and demanding. But my dad believed in public service, in giving back to the town that raised him. He had an amazing work ethic. He saw things through. As a result, people trusted him. Of course, that helped him build a successful small-town law practice. But he would have done it anyway. He went on to help build a community college, and he provided the legal assistance and advice for many other projects that made the town a better place.

Through the gauze of several decades, without the opportunity to ask the questions I would ask my dad now, I may be left to a little creative interpretation. Nevertheless, for me this part of his legacy is clear. Leaders do what they have to do when it has to be done, no matter what sacrifice they have to make. They don't complain. They embrace service. They forge ahead through the challenge. They see their commitments through.

The story of my dad is one of an ordinary man who will never be remembered in history but whose life meant much to me and to others. A person does not need to be famous to be great. Be the best leader you can be. Share your story. Seek opportunities to inspire. This isn't just about building your brand. It is about making a difference.

WE HAVE ONLY SO MUCH TIME

Apple founder Steve Jobs has shared that when he was 17 he read a quote that made him think:

> If you live each day as if it was your last, someday you'll most certainly be right.

In a Stanford University commencement speech, he told the audience, "Remembering that I'll be dead soon is the most important tool I've ever encountered to help me make the big choices in life." Jobs shared that his near-death scare with cancer a few years earlier had brought that idea back into focus.

Here is an excerpt from that speech that speaks to me about the urgency of doing the things that matter, like sharing your values and making a difference.

> *Having lived through it, I can now say this to you with a bit more certainty than when death was a useful but purely intellectual concept.*
>
> *No one wants to die. Even people who want to go to heaven don't want to die to get there. And yet death is the destination we all share. No one has ever escaped it. And that is as it should be, because Death is very likely the single best invention of Life.*
>
> *It is Life's change agent. It clears out the old to make way for the new. Right now the new is you, but someday not too long*

from now, you will gradually become the old and be cleared away. Sorry to be so dramatic, but it is quite true.

Your time is limited, so don't waste it living someone else's life. Don't be trapped by dogma—which is living with the results of other people's thinking. Don't let the noise of others' opinions drown out your own inner voice. And most important, have the courage to follow your heart and intuition. They somehow already know what you truly want to become. Everything else is secondary.

I wish you great success. Build your brand. Do great work. Leave a legacy. Here's a final thought:

This is the beginning of a new day. You have been given this day to use as you will. You can waste it or use it for good. What you do today is important because you are exchanging a day of your life for it. When tomorrow comes, this day will be gone forever. In its place is something you have left behind . . . let it be something good.

—Anonymous

CHAPTER SUMMARY

- Now is the time to start building your brand.
- Ask yourself, what do I want my legacy to be?
- Many organizations are looking at the stories of their leaders as a valuable asset in shaping the company of tomorrow.
- You don't have to live a big life to leave a great legacy.
- We only have so much time.
- Build your brand, do great work, and start writing your history today.

Index

Suzanne Bates, CSP, CEO, Bates Communications, Inc.

Suzanne Bates is an executive coach, author, Certified Speaking Professional (CSP), former award-winning television news anchor, and CEO of Bates Communications, Inc. She launched the firm in 2000 after a successful career on-air in major market television. Today, Bates Communications has a team of seasoned consultants who improve their clients' businesses by transforming leaders into powerful communicators who get business results. The firm offers strategic communications consulting, executive coaching,  workshops, and communication strategy to help clients achieve spectacular, measurable business outcomes. Clients include Dow Chemical, Merck, Kimberly-Clark, The North Face, Fidelity, Mellon/Bank of New York, Habitat for Humanity, John Hancock, VF Outdoor, Raytheon, EMC, Deloitte, and Blue Cross/Blue Shield.

Suzanne is author of *Speak Like a CEO: Secrets for Commanding Attention and Getting Results* (McGraw-Hill), which has been a business bestseller since its release in 2005. The book has also been published in four other languages. Her second book, *Motivate Like a CEO: Communicate Your Strategic Vision and Inspire People to Act!*, was published in January 2009, also with McGraw-Hill. Within weeks of its release, the book became a number-one bestseller in books on communication skills, and a business bestseller on Amazon.com and Barnesandnoble.com. The book has received accolades from highly regarded business authors such as Ken Blanchard (*The One Minute Manager*), Marshall Goldsmith (*What Got You Here Won't Get You There*), and Charles H. Green (*The Trusted Advisor*).

For 20 years, Suzanne was an acclaimed on-air personality with major market television stations WBZ-TV Boston, WCAU-TV Philadelphia, and WFLA-TV Tampa–St. Petersburg. She won an AP News Award, and over her career she has interviewed thousands of political leaders, CEOs, authors, and celebrities. As a nationally recognized expert in business communications and leadership, Suzanne has appeared in hundreds of publications, including the *New York Times*, *Forbes* magazine, *BusinessWeek, Investors' Business Daily*, the *New York Post*, and *CNNMoney.com*. Suzanne has also appeared as a guest expert on Fox Business Morning, New England Cable News, CBS Radio, and dozens of other television and radio programs. She routinely publishes articles on leadership and communication in her organization's weekly letter, *Thoughts for Tuesday*, and on her blog: *ThePowerSpeakerBlog.com*. She is among 600 people in the world to earn her CSP, or Certified Speaking Professional, from the National Speakers Association.

Suzanne pioneered an executive coaching program model focused on leadership and communication. The program includes proprietary tools including the 40-Point Leadership Communications Assessment and 360 Feedback Questionnaire, which guides the professional development of leaders. This coaching model has been used with high-potential leaders who must master the ability to communicate effectively in order to move their organizations forward.

Suzanne also developed the Quick Prep Method, the Audience Agenda System, and other tools that are taught in the firm's boot camps and workshops. She has developed more than a dozen workshops including The 7 Elements of Executive Presence, Powerful Presentation Skills, Leading Great Meetings, Your Communication Style, and How to Give Great Media Interviews.

Suzanne is an active member of many organizations. She is the 2010–2011 president of the New England Chapter of the National

Speakers Association, a member of the CEO Club of Boston College, and a member of the Women Presidents Organization. She is past president of the Massachusetts Women's Political Caucus and currently on the board of The Girl Scouts of Eastern Massachusetts. Suzanne earned a B.S. in Radio-TV Journalism from the University of Illinois. She lives in Wellesley, Massachusetts, with her husband and daughter.